THE
BALTIMORE
PRINCIPLES

CARL DOUGLAS

THE BALTIMORE PRINCIPLES
by CARL DOUGLAS

An Historical Publishing project of the *Arnett Institute, Inc*, a 501(c)(3) non-profit corporation, Mesa, Arizona.
©2011, all rights reserved

ISBN: 978-0-9836152-9-3
Library of Congress Control Number: 2010942684
Printed in the United States of America

Layout, formatting, graphics and design by David Arnett, dba *PunkinRoller Publishing Services*.

Cover design features a modification of Howard Chandler Christy's painting *Signing of the Constitution* depicting the 1778 Constitutional Convention, commissioned in 1939 and hanging in the House wing of the east stairway of the United States Capitol.

www.ArnettInstitute.org
www.BaltimorePrinciples.com
www.PunkinRoller.com

v6.150928

TABLE OF CONTENTS

66 Those who cannot remember the past are condemned to repeat it."

— George Santayana, *Life of Reason, 1905*

66 Those who take the time to meticulously study the past just might discover something that desperately needs to be repeated."

— Carl Douglas, *The Baltimore Principles, 2011*

PREFACE: *"Hey, look what I found!"*

Early in 2010, I was examining the differences in our government before and after the 17th Amendment was ratified in 1913. Out of curiosity, I decided to take a peek at our colonial legislatures to see what those buffoons did. I say "buffoons" because I really expected to find colonial forms of government to be dreadfully substandard in comparison. It surprised me to discover they weren't buffoons at all. In some respects the colonies actually had *better* structures of government than what emerged when they became states.

I had no intentions of writing a book until I discovered these forgotten basic principles that were fundamental in creating this great nation. To my knowledge these principles have no name and, since I do believe I am the first to have put these principles together, I've assumed a discoverer's right to name them the *Baltimore Principles,* after Lord Baltimore of Maryland who first introduced them in 1650.

My discovery reminds me of something that happened during the gold rush of 1849. Tens of thousands of prospectors passed through Nevada on their way to California. Once they had crossed the Great Basin and entered the mountains along the present day Nevada-California border, they immediately fanned out to look for gold, hoping to successfully end their journey there. After all, they would have no reason to continue on if they could strike it rich on the eastern side of the Sierras. They did, indeed, find some gold, but it was embedded in an abundance of what they called "damned blue stuff" which made extracting the gold completely unprofitable.

Ten years later, many of the 49ers passed through Nevada again heading back home. This time they knew more about prospecting and mining and some were determined to separate the gold from that blue stuff. Then one of them realized what the blue stuff actually was. It was *silver*. The silver rush was on and five years later Nevada became a state.

Imagine all those people who had once held that blue stuff in their hands only to toss it back onto the ground, cursing. Because they were looking for gold and not silver, they missed a fantastic opportunity. But even the initial discoverers found they did not have the skills, knowledge or funding necessary to process the silver. Eventually each one had to sell his interest to those who did.

I feel sort of like one of those first discoverers of silver in Nevada. Many people have extensively explored our nation's history, but to the best of my knowledge no one saw the Baltimore Principles and how they became the very foundation of our American independence. This wasn't my first trip down this path of American history either. I have read our history many times but like everyone else I was always looking for the proverbial gold. Although our history has remained the same, this time I happened to see the silver.

Many people may debate as to who was the first to actually discover America, but everyone agrees that Columbus was the first to go back home and announce to the world, "Look what I found!" Even though his shortcut to Asia was blocked by an unexpected new world, it was his announcement that changed history.

I am just a guy who found something that was hiding in plain sight all along. Like the discovery Columbus made and the discoverers of Nevada silver, it will take others to do something with my find. I look forward to the opinions of historians, professors, scholars and even politicians. While I know they can't renounce the history presented here because it is too well documented, I do expect them to shed additional light on this subject.

Certainly I can't be the first to have discovered the Baltimore Principles. I've searched for books and materials written by historians and scholars but could not find anything anywhere. It won't surprise me if a book does surface later on. But since I wasn't finding anything, I was compelled to write this book and say to everyone, *"Hey, look what I found!"*

It was the application of these Baltimore Principles that created the best constitutional government the world has ever seen. Sad to say, some of these solid principles have been forgotten in all levels of our government and need to be revived. What still remain have become so muddied that they are almost nonexistent. I believe that once people understand what these principles are, then *we the people* can take the proper steps toward permanently fixing our local, county, state and federal governments.

As any medical doctor will tell you, they cannot cure a patient by treating their symptoms, but seek to identify and treat the disease instead. This holds true in government, as well. If we are to cure what is ailing America, we must treat the cause. We can do this by reapplying the Baltimore Principles at all levels of government. This is our penicillin. Once injected, the painful symptoms will start to go away.

This book was written to explain exactly what the Baltimore Principles are and why they are essential. You'll learn how these principles evolved and how most of them were lost. Once you fully understand these things, you'll know what needs to be done.

I've endeavored to keep the subject matter short and to the point in this book, so it can be read and understood rather quickly. I have merely highlighted the important bits and pieces of history which led to the creation and demise of the Baltimore Principles. My presentation is a rhapsody of bits and pieces which kind of jump around from place to place, but I felt I had to write it this way in order to properly connect all the dots.

I do express some of my personal interpretations throughout this book. However, when I do, I clearly point out what is and is not historical fact.

Do not feel bad if you don't already know this old history because much of this is simply not taught in schools. But all of it is fairly easy to uncover online. Search the web using the key words and phrases used in this text and you'll find a number of sources supporting the facts and histories I have cited here.

CARL DOUGLAS

66 Tell me and I forget. Teach me and I remember. Involve me and I learn."

— Benjamin Franklin

CHAPTER ONE:
THE BALTIMORE PRINCIPLES

The year was 1650. Cecil Calvert, aka Lord Baltimore, owner and proprietor of the colony of Maryland, was cornered into a dangerous position. The first two of the English Civil Wars had ended and Lord Baltimore, who was living in London, found himself on more than one losing side. He was a Royalist. King Charles had not only lost the war but had been beheaded by Parliament the year before. Lord Baltimore was Catholic and the Puritans had recently won control of Parliament and the English government. Lord Baltimore was Irish and Ireland had lost their rebellion during the civil wars, as well. If all of these things weren't bad enough, the dead king's son, Charles II, was up in Scotland planning a new offensive to reclaim his father's throne.

The Calvert family wasn't Irish per se, but they did own thousands of acres in Ireland. Although the title of *Baron of Baltimore* was under the kingdom of Ireland, their family roots were definitely English, as they maintained a wealthy estate in Yorkshire. To say that Lord Baltimore was Irish is therefore both true and false.

Surviving the 1640s in England required all the diplomatic skills Lord Baltimore had, but now he had to pull a rabbit out of his hat or he, too, could lose everything including his life. The year before, he had appointed a Protestant governor to oversee his Maryland colony. That helped ease the tension at home, but it wasn't enough. During that same year he imposed a new law in Maryland which guaranteed religious tolerance for all of his Christian citizens. That helped, but he was still considered to be a threat to Parliament. It was obvious he was going to lose his colony, so he decided to give his subjects a government that would protect their individual liberties.

In 1650 he introduced a new structure and system of government for his Maryland colony – what I have named the *Baltimore Principles* – which was ground-breaking beyond anything Parliament or the world could have possibly imagined. A couple years later Oliver Cromwell took Maryland away from him and made it his Royal Colony, meaning it now belonged to the Commonwealth of England. But Lord Baltimore got his colony back again when King Charles II took the throne in 1660.

These Baltimore Principles quickly spread to the other colonies and for the next 125 years this revolutionary system allowed them to raise and spend their own taxes, with no tax money going to Parliament.

Lord Baltimore introduced the idea of government having separate branches. His new system of checks and balances prevented any individual or self-interest group from becoming too powerful. His new system of *vertical* checks and balances limited the powers granted to all levels of government. His new structure kept all government spending to a minimum by exclusively granting those powers to the legislative bodies. The Baltimore Principles gave Americans new freedoms and liberties that no other government in the history of the world had ever provided to their citizens. These principles made the American colonies a true land of opportunity and prosperity. They are what became the fundamental cornerstone and framework for our very own US Constitution.

What Lord Baltimore did literally changed the world forever, although very few know this or give him credit. History credits our Founding Fathers instead. We are led to believe that they alone invented the great American experiment. The truth is they applied the Baltimore Principles, perfected by their grandfathers, which had passed all the rigorous tests during the 125 years leading up to the Revolution; not to take anything away from our Founding Fathers, for they were exceptional men. Let's just say they were certainly smart enough to apply the solid principles which had been proven to work every time.

But America has forgotten the very principles which made her great. By discarding these principles we've created many problems for ourselves. Our government has gotten out of control. It's gotten too big and has allowed individuals and self-interest groups to become too powerful. Our taxes and spending have become beyond excessive. Our individual liberties are being reduced more and more every day.

WHAT ARE THE BALTIMORE PRINCIPLES?

*P*araphrased in plain English, here are the Baltimore Principles.

1) *Each and every level of government is to be created by the people, for the people.*

2) *Each level of government needs to have three separate branches; the executive, legislative and judicial branches. There must be an effective system of checks and balances between the branches of government.*

3) *With the exception of local governments, each legislative body has two houses; an upper house and a lower house. The members of the upper house represent the governments directly below them while the members of the lower house represent the citizens within the same region.*

4) *The powers delegated to each level of government are limited by the citizens and the governmental bodies underneath it.*

5) *Only the legislative branch has the power to levy taxes and to say how public money is to be spent.*

*H*ere are the Baltimore Principles again, along with some detailed explanation.

1) *Each and every level of government is to be created by the people, for the people.*

It is debatable whether or not Lord Baltimore himself created this principle. On the one hand he did rule Maryland, but on the other he did give his colony's legislature to the people. Earlier under his brother, Leonard Calvert, the first governor of Maryland, the people were allowed to form their own county governments to suit their needs. This was revolutionary, as all other counties had all been formed for administrative purposes by upper levels of government. Lord

Baltimore's actions seem to illustrate that he at least had an active hand in the implementation of this principle, if not in its conceptualization.

While our US government was created by the people, that doesn't mean all of our governments were. We do have a number of governments, especially county governments, which were not created by the people. For example, the county I live in was created as an administrative arm of the state and not by the communities and their citizens.

2) ***Each level of government needs to have three separate branches; the executive, legislative and judicial branches. There must be an effective system of checks and balances between the branches of government.***

This is one principle we haven't completely lost. But because we have lost some of the other principles there are times when we experience a momentary lapse in regard to this one. For example, when one political party gains control of the executive branch as well as both houses, then the separation of the two branches and/or houses can become blurred or nonexistent. In other words, there are times when we experience a breakdown with our system of horizontal checks and balances because we have allowed self-interest groups to act where they don't belong. When all of the Baltimore Principles are applied, self-interest groups can *never* get control of the senate and thus the checks and balances always remain intact.

We do have many county and city government structures whose branches aren't completely separate because some of the leaders act as both executive administrators and legislators. For example, in my county we don't have a county commissioner, president or chief acting as the top dog to run the county. Instead we have a five-member Board of Supervisors running the county who also serve as our county legislature. This represents a potential conflict of interest.

3) ***With the exception of local governments, each legislative body has two houses; an upper house and a lower house. The members of the upper house represent the governments directly below them while the members of the lower house represent the citizens within the same region.***

This is one principle we have definitely lost. Yes, it's true that some of our governments do have two houses, but there aren't any upper houses existing for the purpose of representing the lower levels of government. Lord Baltimore's two-house system was designed to keep all levels of government from becoming too big, too independent and out of touch with the people. Instead, we have two houses made up of the same kind of representation elected by the same people.

What needs to be stressed here is the structure and purpose of the upper houses. This principle not only provides the horizontal checks and balances between the two houses and other branches but provides the much needed *vertical* checks and balances up and down the various levels of government. Because we have lost this one, no community government has a voice in their county government, no county government has a voice in their state government, and no state government has a voice in our federal government.

Instead, we have four levels of government operating independently from each other and any cooperation is either voluntary or imposed from the top down, rather than from the bottom up. This lost principle has allowed our various governmental bodies to be controlled by self-interest groups instead. Most of our nation's problems never would have surfaced had this principle not been lost.

We have kept our lower houses to serve as direct representatives of the people and the number of seats per state is based on population. This wasn't intended to give the more populated states a stronger voice (although it does) but was designed to give each citizen greater accessibility to his representative.

4) *The powers delegated to each level of government are limited by the citizens and the governmental bodies underneath it.*

For the same reasons explained in the earlier principle, we have lost this principle, too. None of our levels of government has a voice in the one just above it and, therefore, none of them has the power to limit it. Instead, we are held hostage to our elected politicians and their respective parties.

The idea behind appointed representation in all upper houses is not only to provide them a voice, but to serve as a vertical system of checks and balances. This keeps each level of government accountable to the other levels beneath. This is the missing key to limiting the powers granted to each and every level of government.

Again, using my residence as an example, my city's government doesn't have a voice in our county government and my county's government doesn't have a voice in my state legislature. And no state government has a voice in our federal government. None of the levels of government serving me has the power to limit the actions of a higher level of government. Without a vertical system of checks and balances, each level can, and does, assume powers not granted to them. About the only way a lower government can try to limit powers assumed by another level is to file a lawsuit.

5) *Only the legislative branch has the power to levy taxes and to say how public money is to be spent.*

It sounds as if we still use this principle but one has to wonder. The idea behind this principle is to keep spending under control and to prevent wasteful spending. Our governments have put together some departments and agencies with self-regulating rules which allow them to increase licenses, fees, penalties and even some taxes, although they aren't always called taxes. Our politicians have created regulatory positions to oversee departments and have allowed them to make changes without the consent of the legislature to which they should be answerable.

When all of the above principles are applied, we will *always* have limited governments with limited spending while retaining most of our individual liberties.

With the Baltimore Principles in place throughout the entire nation, each local government would have their very own representative in the upper house of their county legislature, casting votes on *their* behalf as instructed by *them*. The county is simply not going to get *any* additional powers without the local governments and their citizens giving it to them willingly. The same applies to the relationship between the county and the state legislatures, and the state legislatures and the US Congress.

Power would be granted *from the bottom up* to the lowest level of government possible to get a job done. This would place a great deal of importance on the quality of people elected on the community level, for truly no votes would *ever* be cast on the floor of the US Senate without the consent and approval of the majority of City Councils from across the nation.

LEGISLATIVE
BODIES
NATIONWIDE
UNDER
THE
BALTIMORE
PRINCIPLES

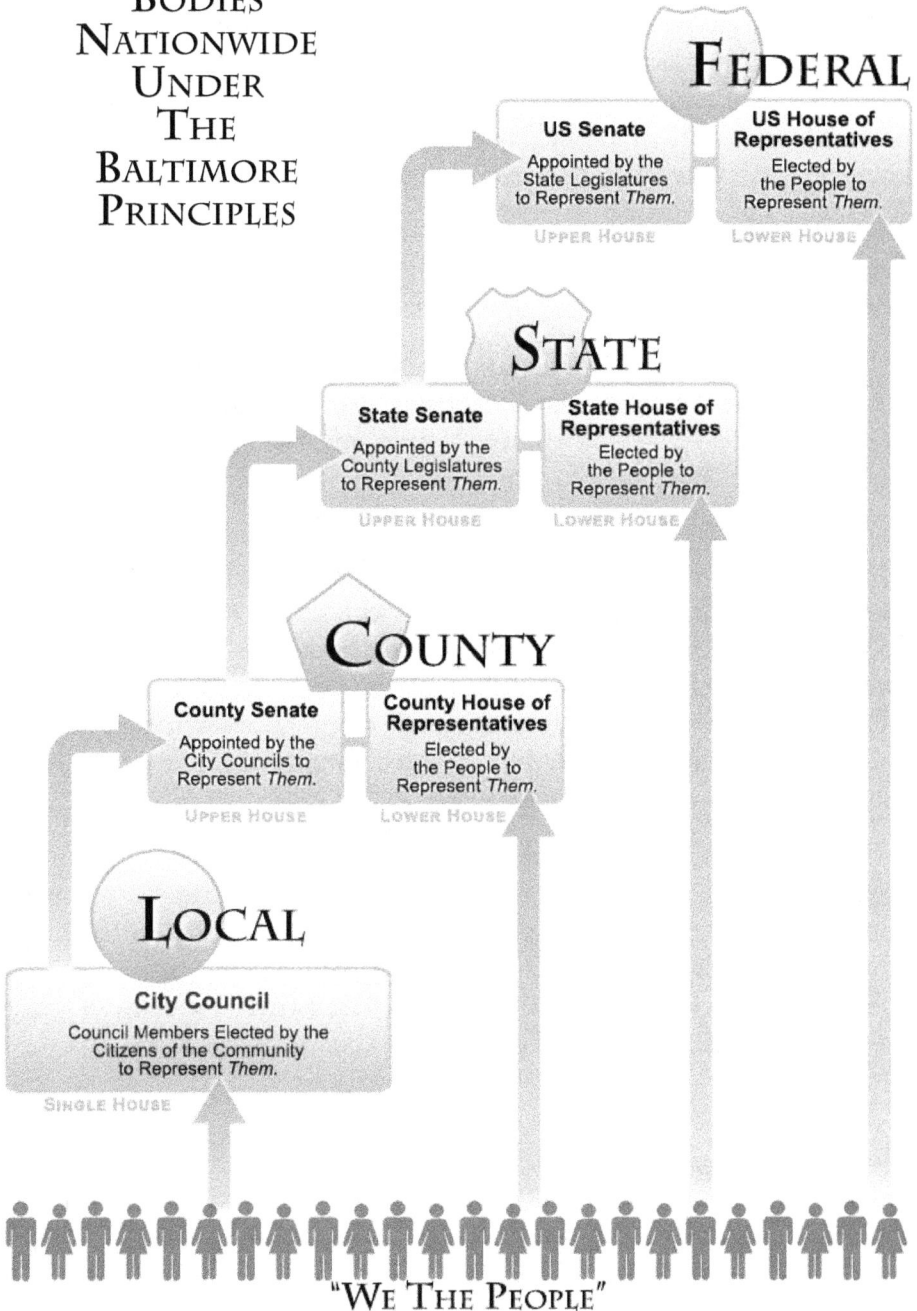

FEDERAL

US Senate

Appointed by the
State Legislatures
to Represent *Them.*

UPPER HOUSE

**US House of
Representatives**

Elected by
the People to
Represent *Them.*

LOWER HOUSE

STATE

State Senate

Appointed by the
County Legislatures
to Represent *Them.*

UPPER HOUSE

**State House of
Representatives**

Elected by
the People to
Represent *Them.*

LOWER HOUSE

COUNTY

County Senate

Appointed by the
City Councils to
Represent *Them.*

UPPER HOUSE

**County House of
Representatives**

Elected by
the People to
Represent *Them.*

LOWER HOUSE

LOCAL

City Council

Council Members Elected by the
Citizens of the Community
to Represent *Them.*

SINGLE HOUSE

"WE THE PEOPLE"

15

The upper house of each level would be *subservient* to the upper house of the level beneath. This form of representational government was proven very effective in colonial America and could do so again today.

We all have an ego, some more than others, but we all have one. Politicians have to have a fairly large ego or they wouldn't even run for office. Once elected, most of them will find their power to be very intoxicating. This is only human nature and to say otherwise would be lying to oneself. Of course, when a politician gets infected with *Robespierre Syndrome* they need to be voted out.

Robespierre, of course, was one of the leaders of the French Revolution who started out extremely benevolent, but became one of the absolute worst dictators of all time when the intoxicating power went to his head.

With this said, all of us are reluctant to yield our individual powers to others. But we find ourselves needing to give up some in order to create a better life for ourselves. We yield quite a bit to our local government so we can have better schools, roads, utilities, law enforcement, etc. To run our communities we elect a mayor and a city council, but we give them limited powers.

Every mayor and city council likes the power given to them by the citizens and is very reluctant to give up any of that power to upper levels of government. So when any upper level government wants to take over certain projects, the community leaders will resist unless the proposed project would be more cost effective or more beneficial for their citizens. For example, a community might not want the county taking over their schools but would very willing to endorse a county-wide program for handling emergency 911 calls.

This goes all the way up the ladder. The county politicians do not want to yield any of their powers to the state government and the state leaders certainly don't want to give up anything to the federal government unless it is deemed to be absolutely necessary. To make a *vertical* system of checks and balances work effectively, each level of government *must* have their own representative (voice) in the upper house chamber of the legislative body directly above them.

66 The basis of our political system is the right of the people to make and to alter their constitutions of government."

— George Washington, *Farewell Address, 1796*

CHAPTER TWO: THE EVOLUTION OF THE BALTIMORE PRINCIPLES

To fully understand the Baltimore Principles we need to review how they evolved. This chapter highlights the historical events that led up to the Baltimore Principles and discusses how they shaped the American colonies and, subsequently, our nation.

PARLIAMENT — THE ORIGINAL TWO-HOUSE SYSTEM

We were taught that our two-house or bicameral congress was inspired by the British Parliament. But was it?

Most kings (of any country) throughout history had a council and so did the kings of medieval England. The British trace the origins of their parliament to the Anglo-Saxon kings who had an advisory council called the *Witenagemot* (meeting of wise men). To accommodate the feudal system, William the Conqueror had a similar arrangement called the *Curia Regis,* latin for "meeting house of the king," "court of the king" or "senate of the king." Take your pick. Some historians refer to it as the "King's Council" or the "Great Council."

Determining how these council memberships were made up really depended on the king and the year, because it changed from

17

time to time. The early councils began with only the king's lords and high ranking clergy, but later the council added to its membership some noblemen and wealthy landowners, knights of the shires, and burgesses. The king's lords are like lesser kings, each with a small kingdom of their own, or one might think of these as being states. The knights of the shires (counties) were representatives of the shires and the burgesses represented the boroughs (some cities and towns had borough status).

In 1215 King John was forced to sign the *Magna Carta* (Great Charter). He only signed it to get the people off his back and had no intention of honoring it. Although this paper made little difference at the time, it would become one of the most important documents in world history. Much like how our Declaration of Independence had proclaimed that "all men are created equal" yet it would be many decades before slavery would be abolished and another hundred years for civil rights to be guaranteed. But the words were there and eventually they did come to mean something.

One immediate difference the Magna Carta did make, was that it created a new law saying that all taxes had to be approved by the Great Council. This was the first time *any* power had legally been taken away from the king. The Magna Carta also referred to the Great Council as the *Parliamentum* (from the French word *paler*, meaning to talk or to speak) and the name forever stuck. By the way, although it was a French word, France had yet to create a parliament for themselves.

By 1295 the Parliamentum was overhauled by King Edward I, and renamed the *Model Parliament*. This added more representatives and it gave Parliament a little more power. They continued to meet in one house until 1341 when King Edward III divided it into two houses, the *House of Lords* and the *House of Commons*. His reasoning for doing so was that there were times when the king needed to address certain issues with just his lords that didn't concern his non-lords (known as the Commons) or he just wanted to talk behind their backs. This two-house system was born for the king's convenience rather than being influenced by anything else.

Let's look at what's important for our study and what influence, if any, it had in the creation of our own legislatures. What developed was a system of representation for state, county and local governments within Parliament. One might say Parliament was there to serve the king while others might say it was to serve the kingdom. Was Parliament a system for sending the king's voice downward or was it a system for the people's voice to be heard upward? Or both? If you were to ask any of the kings, Parliament was there only to serve *him*. But many of the Commons felt that Parliament was there to serve the people. Over time, Parliament's powers grew stronger, but at a very slow pace. The relationship between the Crown and Parliament was tested repeatedly until they clashed in the 1640s, in an era better known as the English Civil Wars. This clash had a great effect in building our America.

It's true that the British Parliament did have two houses with representatives. Its structure, purpose and principles, however, were not the same as ours.

VIRGINIA — THE FIRST ATTEMPT TO COLONIZE AMERICA

*T*he history of Virginia begins with Queen Elizabeth granting Sir Walter Raleigh a charter to establish a colony in America. The idea was to create a base for privateers so they could raid the Spanish treasure fleets and to serve as a headquarters for launching expeditions in search of riches, such as gold. This charter gave Sir Walter Raleigh a *proprietary* over Virginia which included all lands between New France (Canada) and Spanish Florida. In other words, he owned all the land and had complete authority over it as its governor.

His position enabled him to pass his title and land to his heirs. While he did have an allegiance to the queen, neither she nor Parliament would have any direct control over Virginia. The charter also contained a clause saying that he had ten years to establish a settlement or he would lose his right to colonize and thus would lose his proprietary and governorship.

The first settlers arrived in 1585 to establish a settlement on Roanoke Island. This was more like a military operation. Most of the men were ex-soldiers and there were no women. The second wave of settlers in 1587 did include some women and children. Raleigh's proposed legislative government was described as being a

General Court, but since this colony had disappeared by the time the next supply ship arrived in 1590, we'll never know how their local government was structured.

Many of us were taught that due to the failure of Roanoke, future attempts to colonize had to include better incentives to settlers. After all, who would want to go to Virginia knowing the entire Roanoke colony had been wiped out within three years? However, if you read up on this history you'll see that really wasn't the case.

JAMESTOWN — THE LONDON COMPANY'S FIRST COLONY

In 1603 King James inherited the throne and soon declared Virginia a *royal colony,* meaning it now belonged to him. In 1606 he granted corporate charters to two joint-stock companies, one to the *Virginia Company of London* and the other to the *Virginia Company of Plymouth.* Historians usually refer to them simply as the London Company and the Plymouth Company.

It's important to note that among the investors were many wealthy and influential people, including powerful lords. Some of these powerful people had a great influence on how these colonies would end up being governed.

The London Company was to settle the southern section while the Plymouth Company was to settle the northern half. Initially their boundaries purposely overlapped with the understanding of "first come, first served." It was also stipulated that the companies could not build a colony within a hundred miles of each other. Both of these company charters called for a self-governing local council but with ultimate authority residing with the king through the *Council of Virginian England.*

Here's a recap in plain English. These two companies were formed for the purpose of finding precious mineral deposits and whatever other valuable resources they could find. The plan was to make friends with the Indians, have them show where the rich mineral deposits were, mine them and come home very rich men. The king was hoping to get rich, too, as he was to get twenty percent. It sounded like a very good plan. After all, this is exactly what the Spanish did.

As far as a voice in government was concerned, these settlers had none. They were employees who signed up out of greed hoping to get rich quick. Although some had bought shares, all were promised some shares plus plots of land after giving seven years of service. At best, those who did own stock had a vote in company matters but no more than any stockholder living in England and, like all stock companies, it was one vote per share. These employees did not own a lot of shares.

POPHAM — THE PLYMOUTH COLONY'S FIRST SETTLEMENT ATTEMPT

*H*ere is a little bit of forgotten history. The Plymouth Company sent their first ship to America in 1606, but before it reached America it was captured by the Spanish. Otherwise, they would have settled a year before Jamestown. The Plymouth Company landed their second group of settlers just a couple of months after the Jamestown landing in 1607. Named after its leader, the Popham Colony is known today as Phippsburg, Maine.

Like Jamestown, these settlers didn't find any riches either. This venture would prove to be a failure. But abandoning the Popham Colony and dissolving the Plymouth Company had more to do with some untimely deaths. George Popham died within the first year, and is believed to be the only death in this colony. This was soon followed by news from England that the brother of Raleigh Gilbert, the colony's second in command, had died and had left his title and a castle to Gilbert in his will. You might say that he had won the lottery and decided to call it quits and return home. Therefore, this colony only lasted one year. The company was dissolved and their charter was given to the London Company. But the Popham Colony did make an impact.

The first ship ever built in the New World by the English was built by the settlers in the Popham Colony. It sailed across the Atlantic to England and then back again to supply Jamestown. On the way back, it survived what many claim was a hurricane while its larger flagship did not. This ship proved that these American colonies would be a great place for shipbuilding.

Perhaps the biggest impact was that the London and Plymouth charters technically remained as two separate charters even though they both became property of the London Company. All future colony charters were granted from one or the other. Those granted from the Plymouth charter would get extra liberties not granted to those derived from the London charter. Also, due to this separation, the American colonies (and later as states) always had this certain north and south division that went far beyond any boundary line drawn on paper.

VIRGINIA — THE DEVELOPMENT OF JAMESTOWN

Initially the local government in Jamestown consisted of a president and a seven-man council. These men were appointed by King James. At least this was how it was in 1607 when the first settlers arrived. Two years later under Virginia's third president, Captain John Smith, the king issued an updated or second charter which allowed the London Company to choose its new governor from amongst its shareholders. Under this provision any settler who owned stock had a vote, but so did all the stockholders back in England.

1609-1610 proved disastrous for Jamestown. All the survivors were about to pull the plug on the whole venture when their new royal governor, Lord de La Warr, arrived. He brought with him some much needed supplies and was able to convince the settlers to stay. Lord de La Warr's leadership saved this colony and kept the door open for future colonies. For his deeds (and there were many of them) he was made royal governor for life. But that only lasted eight years, as he died of disease in 1618. Without a doubt, Lord de La Warr is a genuine hero.

It's from his name we get *Delaware,* a contraction of *"de La Warr."* In honor of his greatness, many people, places and things were named after him including a river, a state and even an Indian tribe.

Although Jamestown was surviving, the London Company was going broke. King James ran an ambitious campaign to sell more stock.

He promised investors quick returns and big profits. He also appealed to English patriotism, proclaiming that such investments would increase the standard of living throughout England. Money poured in, but the promises were not fulfilled. By 1612 the Company was broke again. To make up for his unfulfilled promises of cash, the stockholders were given land in Virginia instead.

But 1612 also marked a turning point for the better. John Rolfe introduced a new, much sweeter strain of tobacco he had smuggled in from Trinidad. The native Virginia tobacco was too harsh and was therefore unmarketable. He had planted his new strain earlier, but it took a year or two to have enough crop for export. Europeans fell in love the new strain and became hooked. Virginia was on its way to becoming very rich. Spain had imposed the death penalty for anyone selling their tobacco seeds to a non-Spaniard. It was clear now that their measures were not without reason.

Beginning in 1618 the king offered the stockholders additional acreage if they would pay the passage for new settlers. Stockholders living in England would get 50 acres per settler (male head of household) while those stockholders living in Virginia got 100 acres. This was called the *Headright* system. The indentured servants were not guaranteed any land under the Headright, but some were able to negotiate themselves separate deals with their landowners.

Note: 1618 is also when the Thirty Years War began. This was a big European war between Protestants and Catholics, fought mainly throughout present day Germany. England wasn't the major player in this war, but they did support the Protestants and the war gave them the excuse to take additional cracks at their traditional enemy, Spain. This war did have some effect on the colonies because the king's attention was often diverted. Plus, it put a huge dent in the royal treasury. The war also attracted new foreign settlers from throughout Europe wanting to escape the wrath of war. They needed a place to go and the Virginia colony appeared to be a very good choice.

By 1619 they were getting a bunch of new settlers into Virginia, but still there weren't enough. Therefore, the Virginia Company dumped the idea of trying to keep a monopoly on land ownership and started offering new land deals to settlers. They also allowed for the development of cities, declared English Common Law for all citizens and the governor no longer had the final say in local legal matters.

The Virginia Company also created a new legislative body called the *House of Burgesses.* A Burgess is a representative for a municipality or borough. These improved changes really did attract more settlers.

Among the first non-English to arrive were East Prussians and Poles. At first they were denied the rights of Englishmen, but after staging what became the first workers strike recorded in the New World, the House of Burgesses gave all non-English settlers the same rights as English citizens. The House also gave all male land owners over the age of seventeen the right to vote.

Another problem facing Virginia was a shortage of European women. So, in 1620 the Company brought over a ship carrying one hundred young single women. It didn't take long for each of these ladies to find a husband. However, each husband-to-be had to reimburse the Company for their bride-to-be's voyage, which was 120 pounds of tobacco.

To think that only ten years earlier the Virginia settlers had almost called it quits. Now Virginia had become a real land of opportunity. It looked as if everything was turning up roses. But in 1622 they had a dispute with the local Indians which led to the Jamestown Massacre, killing off about half the white population. King James was displeased and lost confidence in the London Company. In 1624, King James revoked their charter and made Virginia *his* royal colony. Now *he* owned it. He dissolved the House of Burgesses and appointed his own royal governor to run the colony.

King James died the following year and was replaced by his son, Charles. In 1627 King Charles restored the House of Burgesses and, with the exception of the Commonwealth years under Oliver Cromwell, this structure of government would last until the American Revolution.

The bottom line: What Virginia ended up with was a legislative body elected by the people, while the executive branch was run by a royal governor appointed by the king. Not bad, considering that the people back in England did not yet have anything like that.

THE PILGRIMS

*B*efore we begin, let's review some little known religious differences. The Church of England, as its name implies, is the official church in England. It has been described as being part Catholic and part Protestant. The Puritans were a spin-off of those who liked the Church of England, but wanted to purify it by making it less Catholic. Then there were the Separatists. This refers to any Protestant sect other than the Puritans or the Church of England. For example, the Pilgrims and Quakers were called Separatists. Puritans and Separatists did not like each other. To them religious tolerance meant there would not be any trouble as long as each stayed away from the other.

The Pilgrims were not called Pilgrims back then either. They were two groups of Separatists who fled England, going to the Netherlands about the same time as the founding of Jamestown. Although they were well treated by the Dutch, they didn't like the idea of their children learning the Dutch language and customs. They wanted to leave Holland. The Dutch offered them a chance to establish their own settlement in New Amsterdam, but because they wanted to get away from all Dutch influence, they said no.

At this time the Dutch did have some small fur trapping settlements in America, but nothing like a real community. Also, take note that New Amsterdam did not really belong to the Dutch. They took advantage of their friendship with England while she was engaged with too many other problems. Between the war, a failing economy, a drained royal treasury and several major internal problems brewing within, the English were in no position to do anything about the Dutch and Swedes (New Sweden) sneaking into their American territory. Actually, they didn't *sneak* in because they were quite open about it. The Dutch and Swedes figured possession was nine-tenths of the law. Note: Decades later the Dutch took over New Sweden only to lose New Amsterdam to the English.

The Pilgrims applied for a land patent with the London Company. The Company didn't really like the idea of allowing Separatists to move into Virginia, but to counter the Dutch they needed people to move into those areas where the Dutch were settling. So, they gave the Pilgrims a patent to settle at the mouth of the Hudson River, which was at the northern edge of the London Charter, the exact same spot the Dutch had offered them.

Rough seas prevented the Pilgrims from reaching the Hudson and they ended up at Cape Cod, landing in 1620 at what would become known as Plymouth Rock. But before going ashore they had to create and sign the *Mayflower Compact* because they found themselves in the middle of nowhere without any patent or permission to be there. England already hated them for being Separatists and they did not need to give the king any excuse to hassle them.

Word of the new settlement got back to the king and the London Company along with a copy of the Mayflower Compact. Basically the Pilgrims said (and I'm paraphrasing), *"Due to no fault of our own, we ended up here. We pledge our allegiance to the king and we shall live according to English law. But seeing how we are stuck out here in the middle of nowhere without supervision and without authority, we will have to self-govern until something else is established."*

The Mayflower Compact wasn't that bold or direct, but it did mention that they would be governing themselves. This did not raise any red flags back in England because all colony charters granted a provision allowing for self-governing communities.

This land where the Pilgrims settled didn't technically belong to the London Charter. The land belonged to the Plymouth Charter, which was owned by the London Company. But the story doesn't stop here. Some of the original stockholders of the defunct Plymouth Company were able to convince the king to give it back to them under a new organization, the *Plymouth Council for New England.* In this way, they became the king's governing committee for all colonies in New England. Although no one knows exactly who had the king's ear, we do know there were several powerful lords involved because their names are written on the charter.

The old Plymouth Charter was revised and renamed the *New England Charter.* Its southern border was shortened to the 40th parallel (the present day southern border of New York) and its east-west boundaries were described simply as "sea to sea." At this same time, the London Company's charter was revised and it, too, said "sea to sea." One can't help but wonder if this was the seed for what would become President Polk's *Manifest Destiny.* After all, with these revisions one can honestly say the king had officially declared that all lands west to the Pacific Ocean belonged to England.

The Pilgrims got their first charter in 1621 from the Plymouth Council. Not to be confused with the original Plymouth Charter (now called the New England Charter), the Pilgrims' Mayflower Compact was replaced by the *New Plymouth Charter*. What was amazing, though, is that the New Plymouth Charter allowed the Pilgrims to continue their practice of self-government and nothing was said about having a royal governor or anything. It just said they were now under the New England Charter and that they were to continue governing as stipulated by the Mayflower Compact. Because of the wording, this did not raise any red flags either.

Although the Pilgrims and Puritans did not like each other, the Pilgrims did sell six large units of land to the Dorchester Company, which in turn established Puritan settlements. These unwanted neighbors started moving in as early as 1628.

BACK TO MAINE

*H*ere we are, back to Maine again. Most of us are unaware that Maine was in essence our third American colony. Obviously, some of the original investors in the Plymouth Company had not given up on the Popham Colony idea and were determined to make another go of it. The Plymouth Council granted them a patent in 1622, thus establishing the Province of Maine. The following year another colony landed in Maine, establishing what was to become the third oldest English-built settlement in the US, known today as Portland.

One could say Maine was always a "colony in the making," as it had a hard time surviving. Although more land patents were granted in an effort to build up Maine, she never became an actual colony. She attracted very few settlers and many fortunes were lost trying to colonize her. With this said, Maine became the redheaded stepchild of New England. In 1664, King Charles II gave Maine to the New York Colony. Later, in 1686, she was transferred to the Massachusetts Bay Colony where she remained until becoming a state in 1820.

Given her remoteness, small population and lack of wealth, Maine never became a major player in the making of America. In terms of men and money, she just didn't have that much to offer. But every time New England ran into trouble, Maine would always be there to pitch in and do her part. No one could ask for more than that. You've got to love Maine.

KING CHARLES I

*I*n 1625 King James died and his son Charles inherited the throne. He needs to be mentioned because his reign had as much to do with shaping America as anything. He inherited many problems from his father such as the war, a poor economy, a broke treasury and major political problems within. He didn't need any more problems, yet shortly after getting crowned he married, by proxy, the Princess of France, a devout Catholic. He already had one religious war on his hands, but his marriage gave him a new one inside his kingdom. If that wasn't bad enough, he was constantly at odds with Parliament. To make matters even worse, in 1629 King Charles dissolved Parliament and governed for the next eleven years without any input from a representative body. This really escalated the feud between himself and Parliament. Civil war was inevitable and during the 1640s there were three of them, not counting the civil wars which also took place in Ireland and Scotland. These events definitely affected America, impacting how the colonial governments would evolve.

With every issue there are at least two sides, and since England had several conflicting issues going on at the same time, that meant there were multiple sides during the turbulent years of King Charles' reign. A number of the wealthier men knew they could easily end up on one of the losing sides. Just in case, they needed to develop a contingency plan. But where would they go?

Should these powerful men have to flee England, they needed a place where neither king nor parliament could get at them. They needed a place where they could be free. Some of these powerful men used their influence and wealth to create such a place for themselves in the colonies. Besides, some of these colonial investments were now making good money. They figured if they played their cards right, investing in the colonies represented a win-win situation for them.

These were cloak-and-dagger times during which committing thoughts to paper could lead to charges of treason. Written documentation is therefore next to nonexistent. However, when one adds up the bits and pieces, it is reasonable to assume that these wealthy and powerful men did just that. Throughout history we have seen numerous times when wealthy men have made contingency plans. We see that going on today right here in America. I do not think the minds of the wealthy men of that era were any different than those of any other period in history.

THE MASSACHUSETTS BAY COMPANY

The Plymouth Council granted a corporate charter to the *Massachusetts Bay Company* in 1628. The king had no idea what was really going on out there, but the Massachusetts Bay Company was allowing Puritans to settle there, too. The Plymouth Council also gave the Massachusetts Bay Company the same rights to self-govern. The next year, in accordance with the Cambridge Agreement, a Puritan leader was named royal governor and Massachusetts was guaranteed to remain as a self-governing colony, answerable only to the king. This was extended to the other charters within the New England Charter. This meant that all of these colonies could elect their own governors and, in essence, have total control of their colonial governments. Wow!

Sure, this new deal said New England was under the authority of the king, but with all his troubles there really wasn't much he could do. In truth, he had little or no control over New England.

The Puritans weren't the only ones seeking a safe haven. Other groups disliked by the king found ways to get land grants, too. Among these were the Quakers, who were not liked by the Puritans either. So while New England was filling in with settlers seeking religious freedom, the actual practice of religious tolerance in New England was quite scarce. At best, these various sects could get along only by avoiding each other.

Come 1635 the king discovered what was really going on in New England and forced the Plymouth Council of New England to surrender its charter and dissolve itself. But before the council did, they secretly divided the remaining land among their remaining members.

The king thought he could take the bull by the horns, but found he really could not do anything until he resolved his more threatening matters at home.

MARYLAND

In 1632 the king granted a proprietary charter to Lord Baltimore, a title owned by the Calvert family, giving him sole ownership of Maryland, which was much bigger than it is today. Its northern border went all the way up to New York. This was carved out of the old London Company, now called the Royal Virginia Colony and owned by the king. Lord Baltimore was an Irish Catholic, so the king's idea was to create a colony for Catholics. The king made this deal with Sir George Calvert who died before actually setting up his colony. By the way, Maryland was named after King Charles' wife, Queen Henrietta Maria.

Sir George Calvert's son, Cecil Calvert, took over running the colony, although he never went there in person. He had no experience in running a government at any level, but he was an educated man and proved to be very good. Running things from England, he sent his younger brother, Leonard, to personally oversee the development. Leonard became the colony's first proprietary governor.

To get his colony going, Lord Baltimore (Cecil) sold off large tracts of land to wealthy people. Let's call them his *sub-lords*. He mandated that all sub-lords had to live there. He also mandated that every servant (male laborer over the age of 15) brought over would be given 100 acres of the sub-lord's land upon arrival. These servants were required to give ten years of indentured service to their master (sub-lord). These servants were allowed to work their acreage in their spare time. Since these servants were landowners, they all had the right to vote. This was an unheard of opportunity, for both the rich and the poor. In an effort to attract even more settlers, land purchases were made available to Protestants, too.

Lord Baltimore's Maryland began developing and operating like all the feudal systems throughout Europe and, had it not been for a series of events, the feudal system probably would have become deeply seeded. His colony's legislature was designed to serve as the governor's council, just like Parliament had begun as being the king's council. Like all English kings, Lord Baltimore also thought of the legislature as an expansion of his executive powers. They were there to serve him. But between the events that occurred in Maryland and the civil wars in England, he was pressed to do something completely different.

Governor Leonard Calvert's style was rather informal, but not by choice. Historians say that in the beginning he tried ruling in an absolutist way, meaning he was all-powerful. But after one year he reorganized his legislative body to serve as a deliberative assembly, which means that he included representatives for the commoners as well as representatives for the community governments. Governor Calvert realized just how difficult it was on everyone to build a colony from scratch and therefore he had to treat his colonists more like personal friends.

Maryland's first settlement, St Mary's City, was founded in 1634. This, as well as the subsequent settlements, were not laid out like regular towns but were rural towns. People did not live in neighborhoods, but on their farms instead. Even today many of these original towns are still unincorporated. If fact, St Mary's City is unincorporated today and the only incorporated city in the original county is its current county seat, Leonardtown, named after Governor Leonard Calvert.

While each community did have a local government of some kind, they weren't necessarily what one would call full-fledged governments. With that said, in 1637 the first county government was formed to address the common needs; like defense, transportation and dealing with criminals and fugitives. In that same year Maryland's first sheriff's office was established. Sure, there were other county governments throughout the world including England (called shires), so the idea of this level of government was not new. But those governments had been created by the higher government for the purpose of administrating and delegating the power from above, down upon the people below. This one, St Mary's County, was created by the people and for the people. Unlike other county governments, the power base here began with the people and was delegated upward, thus limiting the county's powers as prescribed by the people.

I've tried to find details on exactly how the first government of St Mary's County was structured, but could not find anything definite. I

31

am under the impression that it, too, ran like Lord Baltimore's future colonial government in that it had at least one representative from each community government and at least one representative elected by the citizens of each community. Unlike other county governments, this one really did represent the people and their communities. Think of St Mary's County as being more like *The United Communities of St Mary's County*.

It's doubtful that anyone at the time fully realized the significance of what had been established in Maryland. Perhaps they thought this was nothing more than an expanded local government, which all American settlements were allowed to have. But the idea that the people themselves can create their own central government to serve their needs was indeed revolutionary.

Some say it was Governor Calvert who came up with the idea while others say it was the people and leaders of the community governments themselves. Historians aren't sure who did. Some don't think Governor Calvert came up with the idea because at the time all the communities of Maryland were within the boundaries of the new county, therefore he had no need to create one. Why would he create a new level of government to oversee what he already had full authority over? Many historians are led to believe that the people wanted it and, with his input, he signed off on it. Perhaps allowing the people to form their own levels of government was Governor Calvert's true legacy.

Another thing that can be said for Governor Calvert is that in comparison, Maryland did not have near the problems the other colonies faced. Perhaps this was because of the low-key executive style that Governor Calvert had adopted. However, with the ongoing religious wars in England and the various civil wars spilling over into the American colonies, life was not always a bed of roses in Maryland. They did encounter some tough times.

THE UNITED COLONIES OF NEW ENGLAND

For the same reasons the communities of St Mary's County had to band together, there were many occasions when several colonies felt compelled to band together, too. Often this was done only when a special problem came up, like a war with local Indians. King Charles had dissolved the Plymouth Council of New England in 1635 which had acted somewhat like a federal government. He tried to run the New England colonies himself, but had too many other issues on his hands. So there really wasn't a central government overseeing the New England colonies anymore. The colonists felt one was needed.

During the English Civil War in 1643, all of the New England colonies got together and created the first federal government in America, *The United Colonies of New England.* At that time there were just four colonies in New England: Massachusetts, Plymouth, Connecticut, and New Haven.

Their main reason for creating this new government was to raise a coalition of militias against the Indians. The holier-than-thou Puritans always seemed to have a way of getting people angry, especially the Native Americans. But the New England colonies had other reasons to band together; like serving as a forum to resolve intercolonial disputes and to set up an intercolonial system for catching and returning fugitives. Like Maryland's first colony, this new upper-level government was created by the people and given limited powers, just barely enough to do its job.

Often called the *New England Confederation,* the United Colonies of New England was weak. It was a single council with two representatives (commissioners) per colony who collectively ran the entire organization. There weren't any others serving in the government, like a governor or a judge. These eight men would meet to discuss issues, report back to their colonial governments and then come back with the decisions made by the bodies they represented.

The United Colonies of New England almost fell apart in 1656 when Massachusetts refused to join the Commonwealth's war against the Dutch. But this confederation did prove itself during the King Philip's War in 1676. This was a war against one Indian tribe led by its chief, nicknamed *King Philip* by the New Englanders.

King Charles II revoked Massachusetts' charter in 1684 when he discovered he couldn't tap into the colony's wealth. Two years later his son, King James II, imposed his own central government called the *Dominion of New England,* replacing the United Colonies of New England. Still he couldn't find a way to get his paws into American pockets. The Dominion of New England only lasted three years when King James II was dethroned by Parliament and replaced by William and Mary.

The term *Old Dominion* is widely used throughout today's New England states. The name itself is a source of pride, as the New England colonists had rejected, defied and defeated King James' attempts to dominate them.

The point here is that only in America could governments be created and formed by the people to serve their needs. Or one could rightfully say, the Americans got away with it because of all the bigger problems in England.

THE ENGLISH WARS COME TO AN END

The 1640s were turbulent years in England. These events influenced the American colonies to a great extent, but mostly due to the lack of micro-management by the ruling class in England. But new problems and challenges in England during the 1650s would again leave the Americans to do pretty much as they wished.

The Thirty Years War came to an end in 1648. The English Civil Wars ended in 1649 with the dethroning and beheading of King Charles. The civil war in Ireland came to a close in 1649. Leading the Scottish Army, King Charles II tried to retake the throne, but was forced into exile in 1651. The Church of England and the Catholics lost their momentum, with the Puritans coming out on top.

The 1650s saw a very different England. The monarchy was replaced with the Commonwealth of England (1649-53) followed by the Protectorate (1653-59) under Oliver Cromwell's personal rule. These events did not solve the problems, although some good things did come about. Oliver Cromwell died in 1658 and Parliament could not come up with an agreeable solution to their nation's problems. So in 1660, the monarchy was restored by bringing back King Charles II.

BACK TO MARYLAND

*B*eing both Catholic and a supporter of King Charles, Lord Baltimore (Cecil) found himself in a dangerous position during and after the English Civil Wars. He had successfully tap danced his way through the civil wars, but in order to continue surviving he had to rely on all his diplomatic skills, which he did.

Lord Baltimore, who was still ruling Maryland from England, was under enormous pressure from many sides. Shortly after King Charles' execution in 1649, he surprised everyone when he announced that *complete religious tolerance* would be enforced in Maryland. This shouldn't have surprised anyone, but it did. Actually, it wasn't complete tolerance either, as it applied only to those religions embracing Jesus Christ. But as long as one was Christian, he would be protected by the new laws. Historians say that Lord Baltimore's motivation was because the Protestants had quickly outnumbered the Catholics in Maryland and his Catholics were the ones needing the protection.

Since the Puritans were the victors in the English civil wars, they now had control of many governments on both sides of the Atlantic. Non-Puritans were being persecuted throughout the American colonies. In New England the Puritans had just passed a new law expelling all non-Puritan citizens. These people needed a place to go. Lord Baltimore invited them to live in Maryland, but they needed assurance that they wouldn't be harassed there later on. Lord Baltimore also needed to protect his Catholic citizens from the wrath of the Puritans. Lord Baltimore had a pretty good idea that he was about to lose his colony to Oliver Cromwell. If so, he wouldn't be able to protect his citizens anymore. He needed to do something which would allow his citizens to protect themselves.

In 1650 Lord Baltimore restructured his government in Maryland. His new system was designed to protect everyone regardless of their religion by creating a government for all the people. Every citizen was guaranteed a voice in all levels of government. And the citizens were guaranteed to have an additional voice (collectively) as being part of a community, a county and the colony.

His new colonial government would have separate branches, meaning that the legislature was completely separate from the executive branch (the governor). He gave his governor veto power over the legislature, but in turn he gave the legislature the power to override his veto with enough votes. This was the first time *anywhere* throughout the world such a government existed. His new structure included a well-crafted system of checks and balances, both horizontal and vertical. He also gave his legislature the sole power to levy taxes and only they could say how the money was to be used.

Maryland's new 1650 legislature brought about yet another change, introducing their version of the two-house (bicameral) system. Initially, Lord Baltimore's council was a one-house setup with only his commissioners, but it did grow to include two Burgesses per Hundreds (state representatives) and one representative of the county government (state senator) who was officially appointed by him via his governor.

By the way, the term *Hundreds* was the term they used for *county*. The colony's upper house was known as the **Council** and the lower house was called the *Assembly of Burgesses*.

Lord Baltimore's principles were nearly perfect, but he didn't apply them fully. Although he did create separate branches, his upper house members wore two hats. When the legislature was in session they served as representatives to their county governments but during the rest of the year they also served as the governor's council (cabinet) helping him with administrative duties. This represented a conflict of interest, as no man can serve two masters. The only reason this worked was because Lord Baltimore insisted on appointing genuinely benevolent men.

The other imperfection was that Lord Baltimore wasn't willing to give up his control of the executive branch. He appointed his own governor who in turn appointed (or approved) all positions in the executive branches and all upper house members in county and colonial legislatures. These were known as *proprietary* appointments.

Some historians do not believe that Lord Baltimore came up with this idea by himself. Seeing how he was under immense pressure from his colonists in Maryland and from powerful people in the other colonies, his enemies in England and the new Commonwealth, he had to do something to prove he was loyal to Parliament. However, most historians have concluded that he created this new system to protect the people and their religious freedoms. I concur.

Shortly after introducing his new form of government, Lord Baltimore was able to convince Parliament to grant his colony tax-exempt status. He argued that since his new system empowered the colonists to tax themselves to pay for their own needs, they would never be asking Parliament for a single penny. He also stressed that this tax exemption would attract more settlers and investors, thus increasing wealth on both sides of the Atlantic. This proved to be true.

At this time, Parliament under the Commonwealth was keenly open to Lord Baltimore's new ideas, as they were desirous to create a similar form of representative government in England for themselves.

It would take a number of years to work out many of the bugs, but this proved to be a great system of government. The other colonies began to borrow portions of these principles and created better governments for themselves, as well. Although no two colonial governments were ever exactly the same, the application of these principles were vital in the evolution of representational government. The notion of *no taxation without representation* became the cornerstone of the American colonies. This was indeed *revolutionary!*

Three years later, Oliver Cromwell stripped Lord Baltimore of his proprietorship of Maryland and installed his own royal governor. The Puritans, who were now running Maryland, misread Cromwell's thoughts. They passed a new law to expel the non-Puritans from Maryland and petitioned for a new structure of government. Those running Virginia thought the same thing and asked Cromwell to dissolve the Maryland Charter and give the land back to them. Although the wars were over, there was little peace to be found anywhere. But Cromwell knew the animosity had gone too far. He realized the true beauty of Lord Baltimore's Maryland and knew she was worth saving because no other government could promote peaceful harmony like this one had achieved. He reinstated Lord Baltimore's laws and government and told Virginia to back off.

Who would have thought that Cromwell would be the guy to rescue Maryland? You would think he would have been the last guy to do so. Had it not been for the principles established by Lord Baltimore, I doubt if he would have done so. Shortly before he died, Cromwell even gave the colony back to Lord Baltimore. For the next three years many people would not recognize Lord Baltimore's claim, so in some respects he wasn't in charge.

By 1660 the ownership of Maryland was officially returned to Lord Baltimore. By this time the Commonwealth was falling apart. In March, covertly supported by the Commonwealth, Maryland's lower house staged a coup, taking over the government. They expelled the upper house and informed Governor Josias Fendall they were now in full charge of the colony. Governor Fendall resigned his commission and joined the Commonwealth's cause serving as the rebellion's leader. Although he didn't start it, this coup became known as *Fendall's Rebellion*.

The bloodless coup was short-lived, ending in June. Towards the end of May, Charles II was crowned king. He supported Lord Baltimore by getting Virginia to raise a militia to help him retake the colony. Lord Baltimore appointed his half-brother, Philip Calvert, as the new governor. But outside action wasn't necessary, as Governor Calvert was able to take back the government without firing a shot because the citizens refused to support the Fendall Rebellion. The citizens knew this ten year old government was something worth saving. They knew it gave them more than just freedom and liberties, it also gave them a guarantee.

This new idea of Lord Baltimore's structure of government quickly spread to the other colonies and served as a model to all future colonies. For the next 125 years neither a governor, a royal governor, a king or any parliament could get their meat hooks in any of the colonial treasuries. Nor could they levy taxes upon the American people. They couldn't even regulate trade. Not for the lack of trying, mind you. The English government made numerous attempts. Even when they appointed their own royal governors, they found out there was no way to tap into any of the American piggy banks. This, as you well know, is exactly what led to the Revolutionary War.

At the time, no one really thought much about Lord Baltimore's new system of government and its principles. Even today no one realizes just how revolutionary or important his principles of government really were. As his principles were adopted throughout the colonies, everyone thought it wasn't anything more than a slight improvement to what they were already doing. Each colony thought *they* had invented it for themselves. Many historians conclude that the idea spontaneously emerged throughout the colonies.

The colonists believed these principles were American ideas. After all, it does provide a peoples' government, by the people and for the people. Would any Lord create that? And these principles created the catchphrase, "no taxation without representation." Everyone thought this was definitely an American idea. But according to historical documents, Lord Baltimore was the first to introduce this form of representational government.

They never thanked nor credited Lord Baltimore for his extraordinary vision and wisdom. I don't think he would have cared if anyone had. He only cared about Maryland. He truly loved his colony and always put the interest of her citizens above himself. Having discovered what Lord Baltimore did, I think we need to remember and honor him. But more importantly, we need to understand his principles.

We all consider George Washington to be the father of our country, as well we should. Perhaps we should acknowledge Cecil Calvert, Lord Baltimore of Maryland, as our nation's granddaddy because he certainly appears to have planted the family tree of independence.

CAROLINA

*O*riginally, Carolina was part of Virginia until 1663 when King Charles II created this new colony, granting it to eight nobles. These Lords envisioned building the perfect colony and introduced their form of government called the *Fundamental Constitutions* or the *Grand Model*.

This one was based on the feudal system. These lords would own one-fifth of all the lands. The land was to be divided into counties and each was to be ruled by one earl and two barons who were given one-fifth of the county. The remaining three-fifths of the land was made available to the tenants, who were to be practically reduced to serfdom and denied the right of self-government. The only good thing for the citizens would be a guarantee of religious liberty. As you can imagine, this idea didn't sit well with the settlers. Many relocated deep into the wilderness where they couldn't be found. The others stuck around to protest.

This Grand Model proved to be a grand failure. A couple of decades later it was abandoned. But creating a new workable system was slow because the lords tried to hold on to everything they could. Seven of the eight lords sold their interests to the Crown. Finally, in 1729, at the request of the people, the colony was divided in two, each becoming a royal colony. As colonies of King George II, the people were allowed to govern themselves much like the other colonies. They adopted the Baltimore Principles and became wealthy.

Of all the colonies, North Carolina was the least commercial. But it was also the farthest removed from European influences because so many had been living hidden in isolation. The point here is that top-heavy, overbearing governments tend to be economically sour.

GEORGIA

The land between the Carolinas and Spanish Florida was unorganized with no population to speak of. The Spanish had been migrating northward and it would only a matter of time before they would claim possession. To hold it, England needed to have people living there. In 1732 King George II granted a twenty-year corporate charter to James Oglethorpe who was a retired general, a member of Parliament, a philanthropist and a social reformer.

As a military general, Oglethorpe proved himself more than able. He expelled the Spanish settlers. In 1739 the Spanish invaded Georgia which Oglethorpe easily repelled. By the way, when the American Revolution broke out he was the first choice to command the British forces, but knowing his fondness for the colonies, King George III picked a different general instead. Good thing, too, because I don't know if our forefathers could have beaten Oglethorpe.

Oglethorpe dreamed of creating his version of utopia in America. If you thought the Grand Model was a joke, look at what he tried to establish in Georgia. He wanted to create a colony where everyone was middle class. No one would become rich, but no one would be poor. Everyone would be guaranteed food, clothing and shelter along with land, tools, and provisions. He banned slavery and rum. His ports were closed to all foreign traders. The king shared his vision and authorized subsidies, making Georgia the only colony to receive financial aid by a vote of Parliament. This colony was going to show the other colonies how much better things would be under full government control.

Georgia's government was overseen by a twenty member board of trustees in London who made all the laws. These trustees were volunteers. They were not allowed to own land in Georgia nor profit from the colony in any way.

To find these settlers, the idea was to give those in debtors' prison an opportunity to work off their debts in Georgia. I've read some articles that claim no prisoners were ever sent to Georgia, but I've read others saying that there were many. To be honest, I don't know who to believe. Those who said Georgia was a penal colony have backed up their claims with what seems to be good evidence. However, everyone agrees that the trustees found a lot of "worthy" poor people throughout England and paid their passage.

The *Georgia Dream* was a nightmare. Most historians say it failed because the settlers didn't have any incentives to do more than they had to. Settlers had no voice in any level of government. Landowners were not allowed to own more than five hundred acres. They could neither sell nor borrow against their property. All lands were to be handed down from generation to generation. After ten years they would have to start paying an annual rent on their lands. In truth, these settlers felt they were stuck.

With the exception of the military, all of the government sponsored projects and programs were unprofitable. England found themselves throwing a fortune down this money pit. The trustees surrendered their charter well before it expired. Georgia became a royal colony and the people began to self-govern. In 1754 the French and Indian War began and government money got tighter. Soon the ports were opened to foreign trade. Additional labor, mainly slaves, was brought in and Georgia quickly began to flourish.

The point here is that socialism has *never* worked. Not then, not now and it never will in the future. While in theory it can sound promising, it is based on wishful thinking. And once again, Oglethorpe's Georgia proved that government makes for a poor business manager. While it is true that most of those serving in government are intelligent people and may have proven themselves in business, they do poorly when running a government-owned business. First of all, they are forced to run it by committee and secondly, they don't have the same incentives when overseeing other peoples' money. Seems odd that's how it is, but it is true.

CARL DOUGLAS

THE UNITED COLONIES OF AMERICA

*I*n 1754 Benjamin Franklin formerly proposed the creation of a federal government called *The United Colonies of America*. This was at the beginning of the French and Indian War when most of the colonies had sent representatives to Albany for the purpose of raising militias to assist the British Army. At the convention in Albany, Franklin tried to convince the other delegates that a federal government was needed, but his plan got rejected rather quickly.

However, the seeds were sown and twenty-one years later you know what happened. Again, the idea of creating another level of government (with limited functions) was born out of necessity. As all new ideas are inspired from old ideas, this is obviously how our nation came to be named *The United States of America*.

The main point here is that the colonies were free to form a central government had they wanted to. And they were free to reject such proposals, too.

66 It is hardly too strong to say that the Constitution was made to guard the people against the dangers of good intentions. There are men in all ages who mean to govern well, but they mean to govern. They promise to be good masters, but they mean to be masters."

— Daniel Webster, *1837*

CHAPTER THREE: THE BALTIMORE PRINCIPLES IN REVIEW

*N*ow that we have reviewed the history, let's go back over the Baltimore Principles in more detail.

The Baltimore Principles provide a structural framework whereby all governments, regardless of level, are created by the people and for the people. It calls for three separate branches of government at all levels. It provides a system of effective checks and balances, not only horizontally at each level but *vertically* up and down all levels of government, as well. It provides a two-house system for all central governments; an upper house representing the level of government directly underneath and a lower house representing the general public.

The Baltimore Principles insure that every community government has a direct voice in county government, every county government has a direct voice in state government and every state government has a direct voice in federal government. It makes it so that no one person or group can ever become too powerful at *any* level.

To make this work, though, all of the principles must be applied firmly at all levels, otherwise it can fall apart like a house of cards. These principles are fundamental in creating, operating and maintaining all local, county, state and federal governments.

The flow of power under the Baltimore Principles is always from the bottom up, beginning at the community level. Power is granted to a higher level only when deemed necessary in order to effectively and efficiently get the job done, and is always granted to the lowest possible level up the ladder. The higher levels of county, state or federal government are given power to exercise the will of those who granted them that power. The US Senate exists to carry out the will of the state legislatures, the state senates exist to carry out the will of the county legislatures, and the county senates exist to carry out the will of the city councils, who are popularly elected by the citizens of each community.

Let's further examine the Baltimore Principles, beginning with the order all governments were created, or rather, the order in which they *should* have been created, beginning with the community, followed by county, state and federal levels. I will write these as if they were in place today.

LOCAL GOVERNMENTS

*T*he bottom level government is the city (local) government. Since there are no levels below them, there is no need for two houses. So, they just have a one-house council whose members are elected by its citizens. The citizens also elect a mayor to serve as the executive branch of city government and a justice of the peace is elected to serve as the local judicial branch. Many cities may have districts or precincts for administrative and/or voting purposes, but they are not additional governments. Should a large city feel the need to subdivide by creating an even lower level government, then the existing city council would need two houses.

What is important to note is that in following the Baltimore Principles, all community governments should be created by the citizenry. And I think just about every one of them was. The citizens themselves should determine the role their community government is to play and should determine what powers to grant them. In other words, let the communities form themselves. Such governments should be thought of as being *The United Citizens of (blank) City.*

COUNTY GOVERNMENTS

*E*xcept in rare cases, the next level is the county government. Like the community governments, this level should be created by the people in conjunction with their existing community governments to serve common needs. Most of our counties were created by the state and not by the people.

The county government should have two houses or boards (bicameral), an upper and a lower. Naturally, all legislation must pass both boards.

The upper board members are appointed by the city council which they represent. Each incorporated community gets the same number of upper board members, thus each community has an equal number of seats. The members of the upper board do not directly represent the people, but do so via their community councils. This way, each community government has a direct voice in the county government. These representatives are well qualified, experienced and vetted. This is an important ingredient in the checks and balances system, because each upper board member is held accountable by the council they represent.

Notice I said *incorporated* communities. Incorporated communities are full-fledged governments with responsibilities that unincorporated communities do not have. Therefore, those communities unable or unwilling to accept the additional responsibilities are not given a seat in the county's upper board, just like our US territories don't have US Senators.

I also used the word *vetted.* Initially the word comes from the latin word *veterinae* meaning "working animals." It was first used in our English as *veterinarian,* as a term for someone examining the horses before each horse race. Later, veterinarian was shortened to *vet* and used as a verb to mean "to examine" or "to test." Since then our language has found other uses for it. A veterinarian is one who examines animals. An experienced military soldier is a veteran because he has been tested. In politics, vetted means someone who has been examined and approved by the legislature before getting an appointment to a position in government.

The Baltimore Principles require that each county government has a lower board made up of representatives popularly elected directly by the people within the voting districts of that county. Having such representatives is a horizontal check against those appointed to the upper house by the community governments, thus keeping the politicians in both county chambers from getting too big for their britches. It would be redundant if both boards were elected by the same group.

The other check is that the lower house representatives have to answer to the people, while the upper house representatives are answerable to the city governments that appoint them. That means one board's members answer to a different group than do the other board's members. It would be equally redundant if both boards had to answer to the same group.

County governments are therefore a central government for a group of communities. They could easily be called *The United Communities of (blank) County.*

STATE GOVERNMENTS

*A*gain, all state governments should have been formed by the people themselves and in many cases they were. State legislatures also need two houses, with the senate representing the county governments and the lower house representing the citizens of each county.

Each county government gets the same number of seats as the other counties do, thus an equal voice in the state senate. Each senator is vetted and appointed by the county government he or she represents and is accountable only to them.

The state senate is balanced by a lower house with members representing the general public of each county. They are elected by the citizens themselves. They represent the people, not the county government. The number of seats for each county is based on population. Therefore, the more populated counties have more seats.

And, of course, all legislation has to pass both houses. With this setup, any state could easily be called *The United Counties of (State).*

THE FEDERAL GOVERNMENT

*T*he structure of the federal government is just like that of the state level, except that the two houses are representing states and state governments instead of counties. This is the driving force behind calling ourselves *The Untied States of America.*

Ever since the Baltimore Principles were lost, the members of our US Congress have been pushing their own will upon the lower governments, repeatedly passing bills which force the states to pay for part or all of them without any input whatsoever from anyone but themselves. Your governor and state legislature have no more voice in federal matters than any ordinary citizen.

Your state legislature works hard to put together a budget only to have Congress say to them, in essence, *"Here's a new bill we passed into law. It'll only cost you a half billion a year. How you pay for it is up to you, but you will pay. Good luck."* Since the state governments don't have any direct representation or voice, there's really not much they can do.

ADVANTAGES TO THE BALTIMORE PRINCIPLES

*T*he Baltimore Principles should sound familiar because that's how the US Congress used to function. And like our Congress, the upper houses had additional duties not entrusted to the lower houses, such as the confirmation of appointments made by the executive branch. Before the 17th Amendment, all US Senators were appointed by their state legislatures using the Baltimore Principles. Today they are elected by the general public of their state. That means that none of our state governments has had a voice in the federal government for almost a century.

There are many advantages to using the Baltimore Principles. Perhaps the biggest would be that each upper house representative (let's call them upper-reps) would vote the way the legislative body he is representing instructs him to vote. He is not there to dictate how he envisions things should be. It is not about him. It is about the government he is representing and what they (collectively) want. He

47

is a team player acting somewhat as a liaison officer. The upper-rep reports back and forth, keeping both levels of government informed. Since each level is better informed, each level can make better decisions.

One could say if all he is doing is passing along notes, then anyone could qualify to do the job. To a small degree that is correct. But upper-reps needed to be good communicators with the experience to know the right questions to ask. Upper-reps also serve on various committees, so once again they need to be educated and experienced. The truth is, every level of government sends the best person they have. Many upper-reps during the colonial era had formerly served as mayors, councilmen, board members, etc.

Think of choosing an upper-rep like hiring a lawyer. You want the best representation you can get. You want your lawyer to represent you and your agenda and not his. You want him to keep you well informed, not in the dark. If you feel he is incompetent or should you lose confidence in him, you would fire him. If you suspect he is taking a bribe to tank your case, you would dump him. Why should upper-reps be treated any differently?

Another really big advantage to appointing upper-reps is that they don't have to campaign for their jobs. Or maybe I should say they don't need campaign funds. This alone kept a lot of corruption at bay. Since he doesn't need funds, he is harder to buy or bribe. The only people he needed to impress are in the legislative body he represents. Looking back at when this was done, legislatures appointed only the people they knew and trusted. Usually they would select someone they had worked with for a long time. They knew his character and were confident in his ability. Plus, they liked him.

Speaking of corruption, anytime there is power and money in the same room, there will be temptation. The Baltimore Principles cannot prevent corruption, but it does keep the honest people honest. History proves that when using the Baltimore Principles there was far less corruption among upper-reps than with lower-reps. About the only way an upper-rep could get dirty was to disclose inside information or provide special favors, like a government contract. But, he could never sell his vote.

It is harder for an upper-rep to be dishonest than for a lower-rep because there are more people monitoring every move. With colleagues above, below and on all sides, everyone is constantly looking over each other's shoulder. Using the Baltimore Principles, an upper-rep is under more scrutiny because he has to work with a lot of people who are in the same business, and they can always smell it whenever something is wrong.

If one wanted to be a dishonest politician, they needed to become a lower-rep, the voice of the people. Since the general public has their own jobs and isn't paying attention to political activities on a daily basis, they (we) are much easier to fool. They are not stupid; they just have other things going on in their lives. And this is the way things should be. Since they have paid people (other politicians) to keep an eye on things, they shouldn't have to monitor everything. But when things get so bad that they need to pay more attention, look out! They will vote the bums out. If a lower-rep can fool their constituents and keep their colleagues at bay, they just might get away with a little dishonesty. For a while anyway. Since upper-reps under the Baltimore Principles had to be honest, they were more apt to catch the dishonest ones. I guess it's the old *if I can't be dishonest, nobody else can be either* syndrome. It seems that dishonest politicians rarely turn in other dishonest politicians.

The Baltimore Principles not only provide checks and balances within a level of government, but up and down the various levels of government. The king and his powerful lords tried to build the American colonies from the top down, but using the Baltimore Principles, the Americans built a government for themselves from the bottom up. This was the key to American success.

What is important to note is that the creation of the Baltimore Principles was born out of necessity. Maryland was the first colony in which a county government was created by the people. Some of the communities found it necessary to join forces for various reasons, say defense from the Indians, and determined they should have a joint government. When creating a county, the communities gave it only the responsibilities and authority which were required to do the job. Never did the Americans say, *"Be our master!"*

Individuals are reluctant to yield any personal liberties to their community government, but they will do so if they can elect their mayor and city council and be assured that certain issues will be put to a public vote. In forming county governments, the community governments needed to make sure they weren't creating a monster to rule over them. Therefore, they had to be sure they were being represented by someone of the council's choosing. The people had the same fears and they, too, required a direct voice of their own. In those days counties weren't formed by drawing a bunch of squares on a map, but rather were formed by the communities themselves for the common good.

Some of the colonial boundaries were drawn by the king, so those people did not have a say regarding which colony they belonged to. But some colonies were created out of common needs or because they no longer wished to be a part of the one they were in. Connecticut, Rhode Island and New Hampshire each broke away from Massachusetts. In each case, a group of counties banded together for their common purposes, feeling that their needs were different than those of the existing colony. The Carolinas used to be one single colony. Since the northern communities were comprised of people who had migrated from Virginia and the southern communities had come by sea to Charleston and migrated inland, the two regions found they had little in common and, transportation being what it was, it was hard to communicate. Those living in the south were granted separation, thus the two Carolinas.

History bears out that using the Baltimore Principles in structuring government will always provide the best form of government possible.

66 Our country is now taking so steady a course as to show by what road it will pass to destruction, to wit: by consolidation of power first, and then corruption, its necessary consequence."

— Thomas Jefferson, *1821*

CHAPTER FOUR: LOST AND FOUND

By the time the Revolutionary War began, eleven of the thirteen colonies were using the two-house system. No one is sure how many of the counties or communities were using the Baltimore Principles, but many did. As soon as independence was declared, the colonies began drafting their new state constitutions using their old colonial charters as models. It would appear that they had forgotten the Baltimore Principles their grandfathers had perfected.

One theory is that the Americans got caught up in "we the people" fever and whenever they saw "appointed by" they replaced the phrase with "elected by." Another theory is that since the new US Constitution was being drafted by those already serving in the upper houses of colonial government, they saw the opportunity to cut the leash from their county governments. No one can say why these principles were lost, but they certainly were.

From the revolutionary days to this, no county or local governments have had a voice in their upper governments. Ever since the war, they have had to operate like orphans, powerless to all levels above. The truth is that these lower levels of government had rendered themselves insignificant.

Case in point, Connecticut has abolished all of their county governments. The counties still exist for administrative purposes of the state, but without any kind of self-government within. So far, Massachusetts has disbanded eight of its county governments.

Throughout the US there are some cities that have become completely independent of their former county government, thirty-nine such cities in Virginia alone. There are literally dozens of places where city and county have unified to become one government known as consolidated city-counties (such as Jacksonville, Florida) and the last time I looked there were thirty-one other places considering doing the same.

Why have they done that? Why are others thinking about it? It always comes down to two things. Money and power.

Money is always a driving force for change. Many of these places have simply calculated that would be cheaper. Why have a duplication of services, such as law enforcement, when one would suffice? There are such places where this has been proven to be effective. In keeping with the Baltimore Principles, a government is only formed when the need arises. But should the people no longer need that government or find the need to consolidate, why not? As long as it is what the people really want. Sometimes this might have been done out of greed, one level of government taking over the power and money of another; either a county swallowing up a city, a city taking over their county or a state absorbing the county. I don't want to dwell on who might do what nor why, because each place might have had its own reasons (or perhaps I should say spin). But please be aware that such things are going on.

There are several large US cities that actually started out as city-county governments. The City of Baltimore was the first. Baltimore was given county status and had seats in the colonial (later state) legislature. Today, Baltimore remains a city-county government.

Baltimore and some of the other city-county governments have proven to be pretty good. Other city-county governments might not be considered so. It all depends on who you ask, what they believe has been lost or gained, and how well it fits in with the other levels of government. Much depends on whether it was done because the people thought it was necessary or because a few power brokers had ulterior motives.

Another reason for some of the people dumping their county governments is that they simply got tired of being overturned and micro-managed by upper governments. They got tired of beating their heads against the wall, tired of upper government levels telling them what they can and cannot do. Frustrated, they threw up their hands and submitted themselves to the higher powers, disbanding the organization of their county government, turning all county services over to the state. The story for each situation may be different, but the one thing they all have in common is that they forgot (or more likely had never learned) the Baltimore Principles that made this country great.

Most likely, city governments will always be around because they have to deal with providing services the people can't be without, such as schools, police, fire protection, water, sewage, etc. The higher powers need the local governments, if only for administrative purposes. But it should not come as a surprise if some of them start getting tired, too. Many, perhaps all, communities are getting sick and tired of being micro-managed from above.

Studying the demise of city and county governments in the US is important. The dismantling of those governments can be attributed to the fact that the Baltimore Principles were not being applied. Take a good look, because all fifty of our states have been heading down that same path since 1913. Would you be surprised if someday one of our states decides to throw in the towel, too, determining that it would be cheaper to revert to being a territory again? And yes, I said cheaper! Puerto Rico and other territories have found it to be their advantage not to push for statehood. Why should they?

BUILDING THE NEW NATION

When the Revolutionary War broke out, only two states were still using a one-house system, Pennsylvania and Delaware. This was because they were still under a royal governor. They did not have a choice. But during the war, when all states were free to choose, Pennsylvania, Georgia and Vermont drafted one-house systems into their constitutions. During or shortly after the US Constitution was drafted, all the states except Vermont went with a two-house system. Vermont would not make the switch until 1836.

By the way, Pennsylvania and Delaware had separate legislatures, but shared the same governor. Delaware was officially part of the Pennsylvania Colony until 1776 when our independence was declared.

Our own US Congress came very close to losing its Baltimore Principles from the very start. The Articles of Confederation provided a single-house system with seats elected by population. When the delegates got together to draft the US Constitution in 1787, Virginia, the most populated state, offered their *Virginia Plan* which called for the new Congress to have two houses with seats on each determined by population. This did not sit well with the smaller states who would get fewer seats. Delaware, with their one seat, countered with their *Delaware Plan.* It called for an equal number of seats per state. You see what was happening here? Each state was jockeying for an extra measure of power under the new Constitution.

The heated debate ended when Connecticut offered their two-house *Connecticut Plan,* often called the *Great Compromise.* This one used the Baltimore Principles. I think most of the delegates knew this was the only truly workable plan. They knew this because of its historical longevity. The Connecticut Plan was adopted, stating that all senators were to be appointed by their state legislatures.

We were all taught that our Founding Fathers forged a uniquely original constitution as if everything in it was an entirely new concept. The truth is that they drafted it by using proven, time-tested principles. Don't get me wrong, I really do admire the Founding Fathers. And in the end, they did incorporate the Baltimore Principles and did do the right thing in structuring our constitution. Too bad the states didn't follow suit.

In structuring our two-house system, our Founding Fathers borrowed the nouns *senate* and *senator* from the old Roman Empire. Too bad they didn't borrow the term *tribune* for our lower house. The root word is *tribe* (people) and roughly translated tribune means "voice of the people." Roman tribunes were those representing the general public in government. Wouldn't it be easier on all of us to address lower house representatives as *Tribune Smith* and *Tribune Jones* instead? Plus, the term would be gender-indeterminate. Just a personal thought. Back to our story.

Most of the delegates had their eye on becoming their state's first US Senator. Seeing that they couldn't cut the leash their state legislature would have on them, they lengthened it instead. They wrote in longer terms for themselves. They denied the states the right to recall or remove their own senators. Instead, they mandated that only the US Senate had the power to censure, expel or impeach its fellow senators. At best, a state could only remove their senator by letting his term run out.

If the new Americans had been thinking things through, they should have realized their upper-reps had been vetted when their colonial governments were still vetting. The new state constitutions had removed the vetting process from their senates by having them elected by the people instead. In other words, it was now possible for unqualified people to become state senators and, therefore, it was possible to have two houses filled with unqualified legislators who would in turn elect one of their own unqualified politicians to the US Senate. Can you see why the Baltimore Principles need to be firmly applied up and down the ladder of government? Without them, this became America's Achilles heel.

Our lower house, The US House of Representatives, is equally important as the US Senate. The difference is that this house was designed to give a direct voice to the people. The delegates did not have a whole lot of respect for lower-reps. James Madison called them *theoretic politicians*. American history had proven that unqualified people could easily get elected by fooling the public with popular slogans, unpractical theories and mudslinging rhetoric. These people were not required to go through a vetting process as were all upper-reps. This is how corrupt (as well as idiotic) politicians could get in. Therefore, the lower house representatives were given shorter terms in office. There wasn't much else they could do because even the Baltimore Principles require the public to elect anybody they want based on whatever each individual voter thinks.

As mentioned earlier, a congressman's *accessibility* to his constituents is very important. If a district is too big then his people can't get in to see him and he loses touch. If a district is too small then the House becomes too full and becomes ineffective. The Founding Fathers understood both questions and were very concerned about how to determine the appropriate size for a district.

James Madison expressed the following:

> *"Sixty or seventy men may be more properly trusted with a given degree of power than six or seven. But it does not follow that six or seven hundred would be proportionably a better depositary. And*

if we carry on the supposition to six or seven thousand, the whole reasoning ought to be reversed.... In all very numerous assemblies, of whatever character composed, passion never fails to wrest the sceptre from reason."

At first, some of the delegates at the Constitutional Convention wanted to put a district's population ceiling at 40,000 but many, including George Washington, opposed saying that was too big. Finally the delegates settled for a maximum of 30,000. The first US Congress, with seats based on the 1790 US census, had 105 seats in the House. That number swelled every ten years until the 1910 census when it reached 435 seats. Years later, the US Congress passed the Reapportionment Act of 1929 which capped the House's size at 435, the number that remains today. The population of the average district today, however, is over 650,000 and rising.

The Baltimore Principles never said anything about government houses becoming too big. It just says all citizens need to have their own elected representative (at all levels) to serve as their direct voice. This means all citizens should have reasonable access to their representatives. Is a district of 650,000 people unreasonable? This debate has been ongoing even before our country was born. There's always a pending lawsuit somewhere in the US addressing this issue.

We haven't lost this principle concerning the purpose our lower houses serve. But periodically we do have to question the effectiveness of how it is being applied. Has your own city outgrown the current size of your city council? In other words, have these few positions become too powerful? Do you have adequate representation in your county government? In your state government? Has your congressional district become too big for your congressman to listen to you?

Our Founding Fathers didn't know the answers and neither do I. But when any government, at any level, starts imposing the "will of a few" instead of the "will of the majority" something is definitely wrong. First, we need to take a hard look at how each of our governments are structured. If poor structure is causing the problems then applying the Baltimore Principles just might fix it. But if the problems are due to poor representation, then we need to figure out the proper size for each of our legislative bodies.

DESTROYING THE NATION

*I*t wasn't too many years after the signing of the US Constitution when some citizens began complaining that their US Senators were not being elected by the people. But fortunately for them, many of the framers were still around and could set them straight. But in 1826, the last of the Founding Fathers died. From that day on, radicals began putting words into the dead men's mouths in order to support their own unproven theories. In that same year, before the bodies of Thomas Jefferson and John Adams got cold, the first proposal calling for the popular election of senators via a Constitutional Amendment was submitted in Congress. The proposal was shot down, but the seeds for what would be numbered the 17th Amendment were planted.

Note: Amendment 17, ratified in 1913, mandated that the people, rather than the state legislatures would elect US Senators.

In 1834, Mississippi's US Senator George Poindexter and his challenger Robert J Walker agreed to try a new campaign strategy. In what became known as "canvassing the public" they toured the state giving speeches. But rather than a "vote for me" they each endorsed the state legislature's candidates as nominated by their political party. The party winning the most seats determined who would automatically become the next US Senator, either Poindexter or Walker. By the way, Poindexter lost. The whole idea here was to make the people feel like they were electing their US Senator. This was sort of a spin-off of the way presidents are elected by the Electoral College. Kind of wild, huh? But the crazy idea did start spreading to the other states, some of which began using the Electoral College to elect their senators. Such senators elected by the people are known as *"de facto"* senators.

De facto is a latin expression that means "in fact" or "in practice." It is commonly used in opposition to "de jure" (meaning, "by law") when referring to matters created or developed without or against a regulation. In this case, de facto senators got their jobs by means different from those specified by law.

You might think that the state legislatures would *never* go along with the idea of giving up their voice in Washington. But since the Baltimore Principles were not applied at the state, county and city levels, each man serving in the state legislature was subject only to his political party. If they did not do what their party said, then they would not get nominated again. Same as today.

It should be pointed out that in the beginning neither party, at least on a national basis, embraced the idea of having de facto senators. Or I should say I couldn't find anything on record to support that. But by the 1890s, this did become a major issue pushed by the short-lived *Populist Party*. The other parties soon discovered they, too, liked the idea of the people electing their senators for a number of reasons, but mainly because this would make their party more powerful. Each party would have full control of the senators from their party, just like they already had with all other politicians. Had the Baltimore Principles been firmly applied to the lower-level governments, it's doubtful that any of the state legislatures would have given up their voice.

Self-interest groups also liked the idea of de facto senators, or I should say they liked the notion of the political parties having control over their senators. These once untouchable senators were now subject to bribes. Oops, I meant to say, they now needed *campaign funding*. Self-interest groups could buy senate votes by either donating money to the party or directly to the candidate's campaign fund . . . or both.

In 1872 the first case of bribery concerning the election of senators was reported. By 1913, when Amendment 17 was passed, the number of allegations of corrupt senatorial elections had swelled to fifteen. Promoters of the 17th Amendment spun the stories of corruption, putting the blame on big business instead. They had actually claimed that Amendment 17 would reduce corruption.

One of the problems the promoters of the 17th Amendment pointed out was that each state had developed their own versions of electing their senators, including those states that were still letting the legislature elect them. Which houses nominated or appointed senators? Did both houses vote? Was the governor involved? How were vacancies filled? The answers varied from state to state. There were numerous times when a state legislature would become deadlocked in filling a vacancy. Forty-five deadlocks occurred in twenty states between 1891 and 1905. Between 1899 and 1903, Delaware got stuck in a couple of deadlocks which resulted in a two year period without any senators.

When the proposal for what would become the 17th Amendment was first introduced in Congress, the Senate was quick to reject it. To pass an amendment in Congress requires two-thirds of both houses and enough of the sitting senators knew this was a really bad idea.

The states called for their own Constitutional Amendment Convention and by 1910 almost two-thirds of the states had accepted, thus putting pressure on the US Senate, which now had even more de facto senators than before. The Senate reintroduced the amendment the following year. It barely passed. It turns out the House wasn't too keen on the amendment either. They debated for almost a year before passing it on May 13, 1912. Then it went to the states for ratification. Less than a year later on April 8, 1913, the Seventeenth Amendment became law. By the way, when Amendment 17 was ratified, twenty-nine of the forty-eight states were already voting for de facto senators.

WHAT IS THE 17TH AMENDMENT?

*H*ere, read it for yourself:

Amendment 17 – Senators Elected by Popular Vote

The Senate of the United States shall be composed of two Senators from each State, elected by the people thereof, for six years; and each Senator shall have one vote. The electors in each State shall have the qualifications requisite for electors of the most numerous branch of the State legislatures.

When vacancies happen in the representation of any State in the Senate, the executive authority of such State shall issue writs of election to fill such vacancies: Provided, That the legislature of any State may empower the executive thereof to make temporary appointments until the people fill the vacancies by election as the legislature may direct.

This amendment shall not be so construed as to affect the election or term of any Senator chosen before it becomes valid as part of the Constitution.

CARL DOUGLAS

THE PARTIES RISE TO POWER

*I*nitially, there were no political parties in America. But as soon as one, the *Federalist Party,* was formed by Alexander Hamilton to promote his vision of America, the *Anti-Federalist Party* led by Patrick Henry was formed in opposition. George Washington warned the American people against creating political parties, but since no alternatives were offered, we have parties.

Up until Andrew Jackson became president, parties were poorly organized with limited goals. Usually each party had only one issue or was formed to support a particular candidate. But once those issues had become history, the party would lose the public's interest and would fade away. Even Jackson's *Democratic Party* was formed for the sole purpose of supporting his agenda.

The Democratic Party was almost on its last leg when in 1854 the *Republican Party* was formed to advocate the abolitionist cause. Many opponents joined the Democratic Party because at the time there weren't any other viable alternatives to the Republicans. Regardless of the Democratic Party's position, its members could say, "at least we're voting against the Republicans."

When Abraham Lincoln ran for president in 1860, he carried eighteen of the thirty-three states, which is slightly over half. What gets me, though, is that his name did not even appear on the ballots of ten southern states. Not because they refused to include him, but because he did not bother to go through the official process, such as collecting signatures and filing the required paperwork to be placed on the ballot. Lincoln figured that he couldn't win those states anyway and, with the Electoral College, he really did not need those votes. All he needed was the northern states who had the most electoral votes. He was right. And that alone sure got a lot of southern people very angry.

Don't get me wrong. Lincoln won fair and square. He did get most of the popular vote, carried over half the states and did get the electoral votes required. Even if there had been a more fair election process in place, he still would have won. But it has to hurt people in smaller states to this day to know that their vote rarely ever counts.

As for the party system, the Civil War ended up galvanizing both parties, especially in the aftermath. "To the victor go the spoils." With that said, the Republicans had won the war, too. They were in a position to do as they pleased, so naturally there was a need for an opposition party and the Democratic Party was there to fill that need. During the latter half of the nineteenth century, both parties grew stronger and became better organized.

During the 1880s, Congress began arranging their seats according to political party. One side sat on the left and the other on the right. The infamous party aisle began. Note: some independents put their chair in the middle of the aisle. By the 1890s, both parties had informal party leaders and *whips* in both houses.

As mentioned earlier, neither party claims victory for the passing of Amendment 17. If they did support it, then they did so covertly. Who would want to take credit for hijacking our federal government? But one can't help but wonder if they really did do that. If not, they certainly took advantage of it.

Soon after the 17th Amendment was ratified, the Democrats moved their ten year old *Democratic Caucus* inside the chamber walls and openly elected their first official party whip. Two years later the Republicans established what is now called the *Republican Conference* and they, too, elected themselves a whip. The first floor leaders were formally designated in 1920 (Democrats) and 1925 (Republicans). Both parties elected their first official congressional party secretaries in 1929.

Since the passing of the 17th Amendment, our nation has grown out of control. We are no longer a government *by the people, for the people.* Instead we are whatever the *party in power* wishes. The party system had become our unofficial fourth branch of government and *we the people* have become nothing more than a ping-pong ball getting slammed back and forth across the party lines.

Many historians say the Civil War caused a change in verbs used to describe US actions. Before the war, people said "the United States are..." and afterwards they said "the United States is..." This indicates the US as having become a singular identity. I say after Amendment 17 was ratified we were no longer the United States *plural* but we became the United State *singular* because our states *no longer mattered.*

I want to reiterate the statement I made above that *"none of our state governments have had a voice in the federal government for almost a century."* I do not say this casually, nor is it to be taken lightly. I believe it to be a core problem in our government that exposes the word *"united"* in *The United States of America* as being wishful thinking at best. To pretend that we are united when the word *"voiceless"* more appropriately describes our states is disturbingly uncomfortable, but something we must accept in order to be able to correct it.

REPEALING THE 17TH AMENDMENT

There are two ways to introduce an amendment. One is through Congress and the other is by a special convention called by the state legislatures. Regardless which method is used to introduce an amendment proposal, all amendments must be ratified by three-fourths of the states. First let's look at the provision in our constitution.

Article V – Amendment

The Congress, whenever two thirds of both Houses shall deem it necessary, shall propose Amendments to this Constitution, or, on the Application of the Legislatures of two thirds of the several States, shall call a Convention for proposing Amendments, which, in either Case, shall be valid to all Intents and Purposes, as part of this Constitution, when ratified by the Legislatures of three fourths of the several States, or by Conventions in three fourths thereof, as the one or the other Mode of Ratification may be proposed by the Congress; Provided that no Amendment which may be made prior to the Year One thousand eight hundred and eight shall in any Manner affect the first and fourth Clauses in the Ninth Section of the first Article; and that no State, without its Consent, shall be deprived of its equal Suffrage in the Senate.

Such proposals originating in Congress require that it passes each house by a two-thirds majority. Then the proposal is sent to all fifty states for ratification. The sitting US President is not a part of the amendment process and does not have the power to veto such proposals. Our current twenty-seven amendments were all introduced by Congress.

The other way is for the states to call for a Constitutional Amendment Convention, often called a *ConCon* by politicians and the media. To date, no amendment proposals have been introduced this way. There have been times when a ConCon was called for, but before enough states could accept the invitation, Congress passed a proposal of their own – slanted *their* way – thus beating the states to the punch.

The idea of a ConCon scares the socks off Congress, as well as many individual citizens. It is true that during a ConCon, the states would be more powerful than the entire federal government. Although we've never held a ConCon under our current constitution, we did have one, which ended up dumping the Articles of Confederation and replacing it with the US Constitution. The old process under the Articles of Confederation required ratification by *every* state.

Some fear the ConCon could do it again. But right now there's not one state, let alone thirty-eight, that wants to dump or completely rewrite our constitution. But there are many states that want to reduce the federal government's over-zealousness. The whole idea of the ConCon provision is so that states can completely bypass Congress to make amendments.

Adding to the fear is that there are no rules laid down in regard to conducting a ConCon. How many delegates per state? For how long will they meet? How many issues can they discuss? How many amendments can they propose? All of these are very good questions.

To get a ConCon kick-started, it would take one state legislature to pass a resolution calling for such. Then each of the remaining forty-nine state legislatures would have to pass a resolution to say they have agreed to attend. As soon as two-thirds (34 states) have accepted the invitation, a time and place would be determined. At that time each state legislature would choose their delegates. It really doesn't matter how many delegates they decide to send, because each state will get only *one* vote. Once the language for an amendment has been approved by the delegates, then each state legislature needs to pass another resolution to say how their state is to vote on the ConCon floor. Thereafter, the proposal goes to each state for ratification using the exact same process as if Congress had proposed it. This, too, scares Congress. Let's say forty state legislatures were to pass the proposal, then most likely all forty of them would turn around and ratify it in short order.

As far as how many amendments could be proposed at one ConCon session, the answer is, just as many as Congress can propose in one congressional session. There is no limit. But should the 17th Amendment get repealed and the state legislatures get their voice back, most of the nation's problems can begin to be resolved without the need for new amendments.

Repealing Amendment 17 would be a giant step forward in restoring the Baltimore Principles into our constitution, but it would not fix all the related problems. The Baltimore Principles need to be applied at the state, county and local levels of government, too. Then and only then can all the problems begin to be resolved. All upper-house representatives (senators) would be qualified professionals vetted by qualified professionals. The checks and balances going up and down the various levels would be in place. Then every local government would have a voice in their county government, every county government would have a voice in their state government and every state government would have a voice in the federal government. No level of government would ever be held hostage to the wishes of one individual or self-interest group again.

Personally I do believe that if a legislative body should lose confidence in an appointed representative, they should be able to fire them. If it were up to me, I would include a clause providing for a "vote of confidence" as a way to immediately fire their upper-house representatives. I would allow for any representative, from either house, to call for such a vote at any time.

With a *vote of confidence* clause, no reason would have to be given. Either the confidence in the person has been lost or it hasn't. In other words, no one would have to show proof that their upper-house representative has violated anything or has actually done anything unethical or wrong. However, I would make it somewhat tough, like requiring a two-thirds majority vote of both houses to get rid of someone. Seriously, it would take a huge mistake to get two-thirds of any legislature that angry. That's a lot of people.

In the recent past we have seen some governors and state legislators go on television for the express purpose of begging their US Senator not to vote "yea" on a particular bill. Since they had no voice, they tried to put pressure on their senators by taking their plea to the public. Still, their senators would vote against the wishes of their state. Too often they really think they are smarter than the people they were elected to represent and feel no allegiance at all to their state legislature. To me, that's an arrogant ego that's gone too far.

If states were empowered to fire their senators through a vote of confidence, I can think of a few recent bills that could *never* have passed the Senate without quickly seeing a bunch of unemployed senators in the days following.

If Congress were to propose an amendment to repeal the 17th Amendment, I seriously doubt they would be adding a vote of confidence clause. But how about through a ConCon proposal? I seriously doubt that they would have the courage to do so either.

ELECTIONS

*H*aving studied the senatorial deadlocks while doing my research, I saw many problems that surfaced when states had to fill seats in the US Senate. Since each state determined its own rules, it's hard to generalize all the problems. I did come up with some solutions. However, I do not endorse the notion that our federal government should *ever* mandate how states are to appoint their senators. That should be up to the people in each state. I will pass along a few of my opinions, but only as food for thought.

If all levels of government were applying the Baltimore Principles and if it were up to me, I would have just the upper house of the state nominate all the candidates for the US Senate. This is because the upper house representatives are the only vetted legislators at that level. I would have the upper house narrow their choices down to two candidates, and then invite the lower house to join them for a joint-session vote. Although they are not vetted, the lower house needs to be included in the vote because this senator will be representing them, too. I would not do the old "pass both houses" vote because then the two houses could deadlock themselves. This would work for both county and state legislatures, as well. This plan would provide qualified people to represent the entire legislative body, vetted by those already vetted, and it would eliminate any and all possible deadlocks.

By the way, I don't think any upper house representative should have their party affiliation attached to their name, like (R) or (D). With the

Baltimore Principles in place, it simply wouldn't make any difference which party they belong to because their party would have absolutely nothing to do with how they get nominated, elected or how they vote.

Some may say that it isn't necessary to address how Senators are to be chosen by their state legislatures. If anything, it shouldn't be up to the federal government to tell *any* state how to conduct themselves.

Many historians say that prior to the ratification of the 17th Amendment, states experiencing periods with vacant seats in the US Senate due to deadlocks was no big deal. They argue that since the other Senators were ernestly protecting their state's rights and the individual rights of their citizens, they were protecting the unrepresented states as well. Really? I checked this out and, sure enough, history reflects their point quite well.

FIXING OUR GOVERNMENTS

*O*f course, fixing our government is much easier said than done. First, it will take a massive effort to educate the American public as to what the Baltimore Principles are. Then the people, and only the people, will have to decide if we need to apply them to our various levels of government. After all, applying the Baltimore Principles always begins with the people.

To make reforms even harder, I seriously doubt if either of the major political parties would be willing to give up their power and control over any of the upper houses. Just like it took a third party to initiate the idea of Amendment 17, it will probably take another third party to repeal it. Perhaps a grassroots collective of citizens that feel they've been "taxed enough already" could be instrumental in getting the ball rolling.

There are those who are offering alternatives to repealing the 17th Amendment. One is what's being called the *Repeal Amendment,* which would allow for states to repeal any federal law, should two-thirds of the state legislatures pass a resolution to reject it. Of course, by repealing the 17th Amendment it would only take 51 Senators to keep any bill from passing in the first place. Supporters for the Repeal

Amendment know this, but figure there is little or no chance of getting the 17th repealed.

Many Americans confuse the proposed Repeal Amendment with *Nullification*. The Nullification Act gives any state the right to reject any federal mandate, order or law issued by any federal branch of government if such is determined by their own state supreme court to be unconstitutional. On the other hand, the Repeal Amendment can reject any federal legislation regardless of whether or not it violates the Constitution. The current problem with Nullification is whether or not this act is still around. Some say it's not, others say it is. I strongly urge every American to read up on this.

In some states, there are those pushing to get their US Senators to willingly make themselves representatives of the state legislature again as if the 17th had been repealed. This doesn't require making any new laws. However, there would be nothing to hold these Senators to their word. I guess this idea is an effort to create a makeshift model of some kind. Perhaps they should seriously look into the possibility of electing their US Senators in somewhat the same manner as the states did when they were electing de facto senators. Meaning, the state senate could nominate two candidates (or one candidate per party) and put just them on the general ballot, thus the winner is elected by the people. Such a plan wouldn't necessarily cut the parties out of the nominating process, because unfortunately these two candidates would still have to campaign. They would still need money. But hey, it would be a start and at least all the candidates would be vetted.

Many of the reforms to our various levels of government need to be addressed simultaneously. I think the smaller populated states have a better chance to be the first to apply the Baltimore Principles. Once one state has done so then the rest of the states will have a model to study.

If I had any say, once a state has adopted the principles, but Amendment 17 has not yet been repealed, I would seriously look into the possibility of electing the US Senators in somewhat the same manner as the states did when they were electing de facto senators. Meaning, the state senate could nominate two candidates (or one candidate per party) and put just them on the general ballot, thus the winner is elected by the people. Such a plan wouldn't necessarily cut the parties out of the nominating process, because unfortunately these two candidates would still have to campaign. They would still need money. But hey, it would be a start and at least all the candidates would be vetted.

The structure of our levels of government is not about what I think they should be, but what *we the people* think collectively. I've merely voiced my own opinion and backed it up with my own historical research. You need to decide for yourself what needs to be done.

66 The people can never willfully betray their own interests: But they may possibly be betrayed by the representatives of the people; and the danger will be evidently greater where the whole legislative trust is lodged in the hands of one body of men, than where the concurrence of separate and dissimilar bodies is required in every public act."

— James Madison, *Federalist No. 63, 1788*

CLOSING THOUGHTS

First, I want to point out that the Baltimore Principles weren't used in cookie-cutter fashion throughout the colonies. Not all the colonies applied them in the same manner. There was a lot of tweaking going on. And things changed over time. In other words, just because a government functioned one way in 1710 doesn't mean that's the way they were always structured or continued to operate. I wish there were a book written about the evolution of every community, county and colonial government. But I couldn't find even one.

I experienced quite a journey in researching for this book. I read tons of material including all fifty state constitutions. Surprisingly, I was able to find a lot of information online. Many universities, especially Yale, have made a great number of historical documents available online. Many historical websites have posted bits and pieces of our history online, as well. I learned a lot of things I wanted to include in this book, but I felt I had to keep things short and on point.

I discovered that Alabama has the world's longest constitution in word count. In my opinion it just might be the worst constitution in the world, as well. Their constitution gives all the power to the state government, leaving very little for the county and local governments. The lower levels can't even legislate on local issues, let alone levy taxes. Everything must be decided in Montgomery. Alabama's constitution was obviously not written by the people, for the people, but by the powerful, for the powerful. No wonder there is a big movement going on down there to repeal and replace their constitution. I hope when they do replace it, they will include the Baltimore Principles.

By the way, Alabama is currently on their sixth constitution since statehood. Georgia is on their ninth. Although there are some states still operating under their original constitutions, most states are not. Of the thirteen original states, only Massachusetts is still using their first one.

California's constitution is doomed to fail, for it is way too top-heavy. They have the world's third longest constitution in word count. Although theirs isn't as bad as Alabama's, that hardly elevates it enough to even call it lame. Their constitution, too, is neither by nor for the people and was written to support the powerful instead. It will take some forward thinking leadership to write a new constitution for the people of California. By forward thinking, I mean falling back to the Baltimore Principles.

In case you were wondering, India has the world's second longest constitution.

I also discovered some good constitutions. One I really like is Alaska's. Unlike most of our states, Alaska allows for the people to create and build whatever governments are needed. Unlike other states, not all land belongs to a borough (they don't call them counties up there). Currently they have sixteen boroughs, two of them being unified city-borough governments. All other lands belong to what they call the *Unorganized Borough*. As the need arises, new boroughs can always be organized. Alaska lets their state grow at its own pace, not forcing anything on anyone. The Alaskan constitution is definitely by and for the people. If they were to adopt the Baltimore Principles, it just might become the perfect state constitution.

Unlike Alaska, many states and counties were built for administrative purposes by the higher powers above. This is obvious by all the rectangularly shaped states and counties. Many of our western states were created by politicians in Washington DC who had never seen these places. They did not let the people themselves dictate their own needs.

Some counties don't even have a county seat because they are too rural or too poor. Instead they farm out their county government and services to a neighboring county government. Some counties actually have two county seats, both serving the same county. Some counties have sections of land that can't be reached without traveling through other counties (and sometimes other states) to get to them. What has happened in these cases is that the land, people, economics and geography were not taken into consideration when drawing up the county lines. Had the Baltimore Principles been applied, these counties would have been formed by the people to serve their needs. Such situations would have been resolved by the people from the very beginning.

Another state I really admire is Rhode Island. My dad always said, "Don't set your goal to become the biggest and the best. Just concentrate on being the best." I think Rhode Island has proven his point. There are a lot of things they have done well and they have built themselves a wonderful state. They, too, have dumped all their county governments. I'm not sure if that's a good thing or a bad thing because of the size of their state. It appears that everyone is well represented in the state government, as they have 38 state senators and 75 state representatives.

Having studied all fifty states, I wish I could write about each one. These histories are fascinating. Just as interesting are the histories of each community and county, but there isn't enough time for me or anyone to study them all, let alone write about them. The third branch of government, the judicial, and its evolution is equally interesting. But this book is about the legislative branch and I felt the need to stay focused on that.

I say the best thing to do is study the ones where you live. And when possible, study the others that have valuable lessons to be learned, both good and bad. Then ask yourself what your city, county, state and federal governments may have done wrong and what might be done to improve them.

Our history has proven that by not applying the Baltimore Principles to our various levels of government, the power base has shifted from the bottom to the top. All four levels of government operate independently from each other. If anything, the higher levels impose their power on the levels and people below. We have allowed certain political positions to become too powerful. We have surrendered more of our liberties than we should have.

Ever since I came to understand the Baltimore Principles and its system of vertical checks and balances, I've found myself looking at controversial news events with an entirely new perspective. Regardless of the issue at hand, I instinctively question whether or not the repeal of the 17th Amendment or the application of the Baltimore Principles at the city, county, state and federal levels would have precluded the problem from ever surfacing in the first place. I then examine the level of government that seems to have bitten off more than it could chew and ask myself at what level that power would have been better placed, and whether or not that level of government has assumed a power that should not have been granted them in the first place.

Once you come to comprehend the Baltimore Principles, you too might find yourself contemplating things in a new light. When you focus on the structure of government that may be at fault as opposed to the actual issue being debated, your own mental application of the Baltimore Principles may surprisingly lead you to an enlightened perspective.

During my research I have seen many problem areas that would have been avoided if the Baltimore Principles had been in place. I do believe that most of our problems can be resolved if all the levels of government were to adopt the Baltimore Principles and were open-minded enough to allow the necessary changes to take place.

This book was not written as a *call to action*. This is merely a history book providing informative facts laced with some of my editorial comments in an effort to get Americans thinking, just as any good teacher would do with their students.

But remember that any and all changes do have to come from us, the people. All government levels need to be "of the people, by the people and for the people."

❝Believe none of what you hear, and only half of what you see.”

— Benjamin Franklin

SOURCES

*S*urprisingly, I was able to do most of my research online. I'm amazed how the internet has changed our world. My apologies to other search engines, but Google is my choice for researching, yielding hundreds, if not hundreds of thousands of results from appropriate terminologies or keywords. Thus, validating historical claims for this book was rather easy.

I've categorized my online sources as either *unreliable* or *reliable*. I used the *unreliable* ones to serve as jumping off points in my scavenger hunt for information. These sites gave me the keywords I needed to refine my searches. Once I knew what to look for, I used the *reliable* websites for establishing the facts.

For example, I never even heard of the Popham Colony until I stumbled upon it in Wikipedia. Then I entered that name into Google and found all kinds of reliable websites about it. I even found a website sponsoring a local project in the process of building a replica of that first American ship I told you about.

I know there will be many critics who will say, *"You can't write a book using websites for sources!"* In my defense, I want to point out a few things.

First of all, the history in this book is well documented. I didn't discover anything new. Nor did I find anything that was buried or hidden under a rock. The history presented here is in plain sight and there are scores of reliable websites that back up my findings. All I did was take these puzzle pieces, arrange them and put them together.

Since this history is all old news, I just didn't feel the need to cite too many sources. For example, when I mention George Washington, do

I really need to cite a number of sources to validate that he is, indeed, the father of our country?

I showed my early draft to one man with above average knowledge of American history. When he finished reading it he said, "I enjoyed the history but to be honest, you didn't tell me anything I didn't already know. But what I did find exciting was the way you connected dots. I didn't see *that* before, although I sure should have."

UNRELIABLE SOURCES

Wikipedia: en.wikipedia.org
Wapedia: wapedia.mobi/en

As a starting point, I used Wikipedia and Wapedia, which have articles on just about everything imaginable. Although they appear to be extremely credible, all of the articles are user contributed, so naturally there is a *caveat lector*, or *reader beware* factor. All Wikipedia articles do have additional internal and external links, plus a listing for other sources such as books, magazine articles, publications, etc. From there, I went to reliable websites to see what they had to say.

Media websites

Media websites, online newspapers, etc aren't to be fully trusted either. But, at least they report that something has happened somewhere. But as far as why it happened, I'm not about to put much faith in their reporting. For example, currently there are many media stories about Cincinnati and Hamilton County looking to consolidate into a city-county government. I can take that as fact, but as far as what the advantages and disadvantages to doing so might be, the articles are often spun to support a particular viewpoint. Therefore, I can't fully trust these reports.

The World Wide Web in general

"The Constitution is not an instrument for the government to restrain the people, it is an instrument for the people to restrain the government."

– falsely attributed to Patrick Henry

This profound quote sounds great and hundreds of thousands of websites credit Patrick Henry for having said it, but digging a little further indicates otherwise. The quote simply cannot be found anywhere before 1990. Besides, Patrick Henry, leader of the *Anti-Federalist Party,* was no fan of the Constitution. I doubt that he would have ever said any such thing. Caveat lector, indeed.

RELIABLE SOURCES

Yale's Avalon Project: avalon.law.yale.edu/subject_menus/statech.asp
I found Yale's Avalon Project from one of the many articles I read on Wikipedia. The above link will take you to a menu where you can find a variety of old documents. These aren't the hard-to-read scans of the originals but are transcribed and can be easily highlighted and copied. Each document mentions the names of the major players involved. I searched through these on the web and found all kinds of interesting material.

Yale isn't the only university with archived information. Googling the keywords found on the unreliable sources led me to an abundance of great material on other university and historical websites.

Dinsdoc: www.dinsdoc.com
The dinsdoc website was another place I discovered from a Wikipedia article. This one has tons of external links relating to colonial history.

Parliament: www.parliament.uk
BBC: www.bbc.co.uk/history
As the above names suggests, the British have many excellent historical websites.

The Catholic Church: www.newadvent.org/cathen
The Catholic Church has several websites dealing with American and world history including their own online encyclopedia. I have used these websites before. These articles are very factual and they make no attempt to hide or bury any of their past mistakes or blunders. They really tell it like it is.

All of our governments have websites, but too often they are somewhat lacking. Not all state constitutions can be found online. Few county and city governments will post their charters or summarize how they are structured or even say how they function. But fortunately, I live in a big city. My local library is a good one and everything can be found in their reference section.

BOOKS

I did go down to the library and skimmed through a number of books which did confirm my findings. I could've easily listed them, especially since most of them said the same thing as the online sources. But since I didn't actually read them and prefer to be open and honest, I won't do that. But, here are a few books I found that are worth pointing out because they do offer something different from the norm.

Narratives of Early Maryland, 1633-1684
edited by Clayton Colman Hall (1910)
Charles Scribner's Sons

> This book is a collection of stuff actually written during the indicated period. Most of this book deals with day-to-day living, but it does cover a little bit about the politics of the era. Keep in mind, the historical tidbits recorded here are from the point of view of average citizens. Therefore, what little they did say required verification elsewhere.

George Calvert and Cecilius Calvert: Barons Baltimore of Baltimore
by Browne, William Hand (1890)
New York: Dodd, Mead, and Company

> This book is the story of the Calvert family and their building of Maryland, as told by the Calvert family two hundred years later. Obviously, they had access to family archives and hand-me-down stories. Although it is a little bit one-sided, most of what they say can be verified by other sources. This book is a real treasure!

The English Atlantic in an age of revolution, 1640-1661
by Carla Gardina Pestana
Harvard University Press

> The author took it upon herself to research the relationship between the colonies and Mother England during the English civil wars and the Commonwealth era. She coined the term the "English Atlantic" as a reference to all of the English colonies on the Atlantic side of the New World, from Canada to South America and throughout the Caribbean.

> What she discovered was that a lot of what we were taught in school about colonial history was based on American propaganda and not historical fact. The truth is, overall the colonies had a great working relationship with England. The author found a lot of untold history.

ABOUT THE AUTHOR

$\mathcal{O}$r rather, the *authors;* for Carl Douglas is merely a pen name derived from the middle names of co-authors Paul Douglas Arnett and his brother David Carl Arnett. Since *The Baltimore Principles* is written in first person, it seemed only logical to use a single name, thus Carl Douglas was born.

Both Paul and David developed a passion for history in their college days, with a particular interest in American history and World War II.

Paul Arnett is a retired petroleum engineer and a researcher/historian for the 492nd Bomb Group Association. Paul and David's father Charles Arnett served as a B-24 pilot with the ill-fated 492nd BG in the European Theater during WWII. Paul has probably learned more about the 492nd than most who served in it.

David Arnett is a cartoonist turned computer nerd, having worked in the television animation industry as a storyboard artist for Saturday morning cartoon shows, back when such things existed. His artistic, web programming, book formatting and design skills are second only to countless thousands.

LEGISLATIVE BODIES UNDER THE BALTIMORE PRINCIPLES

The Upper House of each level is subservient to the Upper House of the level beneath.

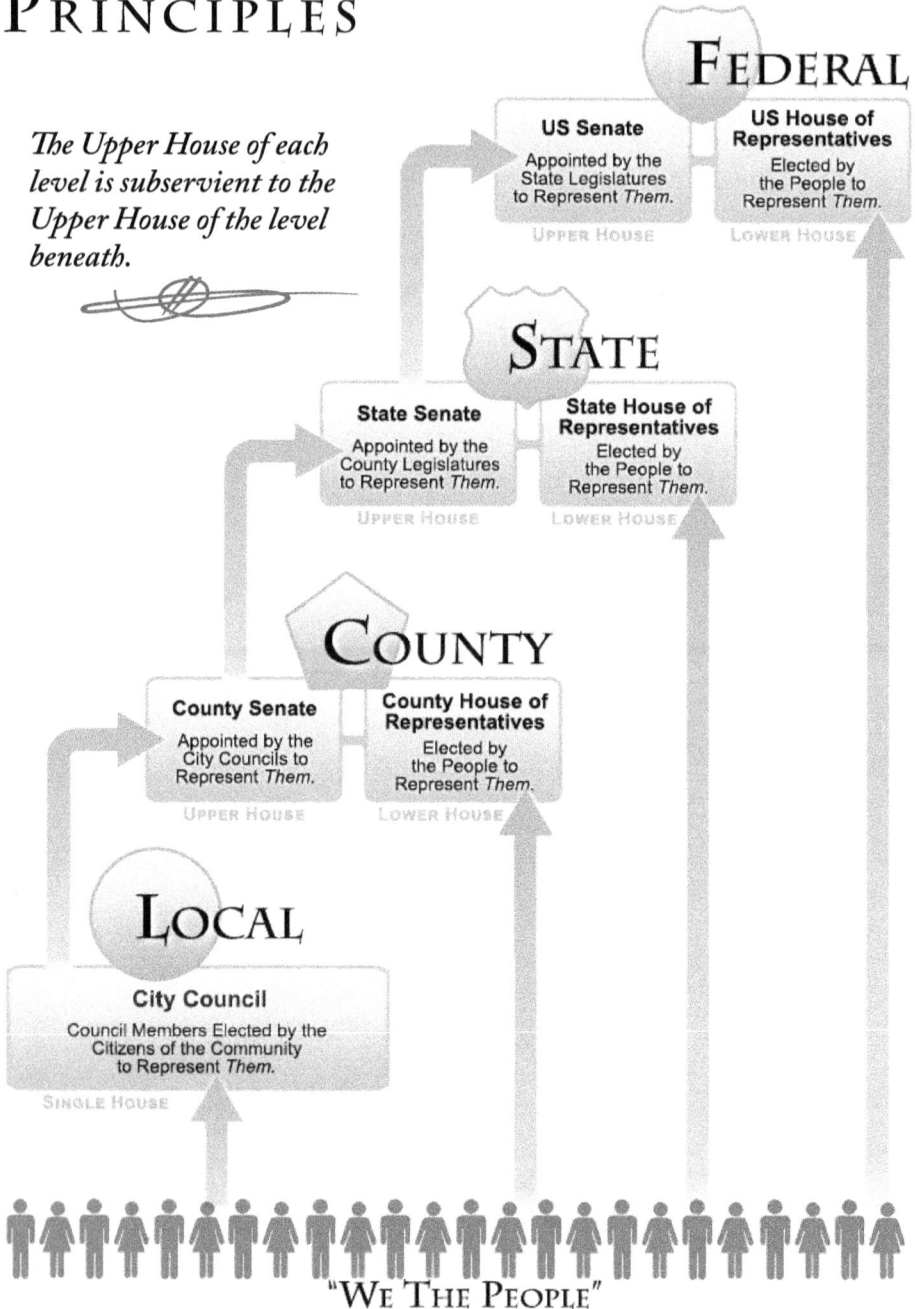

FEDERAL

US Senate

Appointed by the State Legislatures to Represent *Them*.

UPPER HOUSE

US House of Representatives

Elected by the People to Represent *Them*.

LOWER HOUSE

STATE

State Senate

Appointed by the County Legislatures to Represent *Them*.

UPPER HOUSE

State House of Representatives

Elected by the People to Represent *Them*.

LOWER HOUSE

COUNTY

County Senate

Appointed by the City Councils to Represent *Them*.

UPPER HOUSE

County House of Representatives

Elected by the People to Represent *Them*.

LOWER HOUSE

LOCAL

City Council

Council Members Elected by the Citizens of the Community to Represent *Them*.

SINGLE HOUSE

"WE THE PEOPLE"

www.ingramcontent.com/pod-product-compliance
Lightning Source LLC
Chambersburg PA
CBHW072013060426
42446CB00043B/2428